# The Future of Western Civilization

## Psychiatrist Dr Nicholas Beecroft Interviews Visionary Leaders

### Series 1

Volumes 20, 21, 23, 24, 25, 26, 27

## BOOK THREE

*The Future of Western Civilization:*
*Psychiatrist Dr Nicholas Beecroft Interviews Visionary Leaders*
Series 1, Book 3. Volumes 20, 21, 23, 24, 25, 26, 27

ISBN-13: 978-1494340155
ISBN-10: 1494340151

Book design by Maureen Cutajar
www.gopublished.com

# Contents

Contents ........................................................................................................3

Future of Western Civilization Series Mission ............................................. 1

Acknowledgements ......................................................................................7

Dr Nicholas Beecroft ..................................................................................8

Generational Cycles ................................................................................. 12
*Predicting the Future*

Catalyzing Change ................................................................................... 43
*Engaging Emergence*

Successful Nations ................................................................................... 65
*Harnessing the Aspirations of the People*

Resurrecting Christianity ......................................................................... 96
*Rising to the Challenges of a Complex World*

German Identity & Patriotism ................................................................ 113
*Healing the Wounds, Integrating the Shadow*

Compassionate Healthcare .................................................................... 136
*Re-humanising Medicine*

New Money ............................................................................................ 173
*The Evolution of Finance*

Other Books in the Series ...................................................................... 196

Contact & Social Media ......................................................................... 198

Write a review ....................................................................................... 199

# Future of Western Civilization Series Mission

I'm Dr Nicholas Beecroft, a Consultant Psychiatrist in London. I'm exploring the Future of Western Civilization through a series of interviews. I want us to rejuvenate our energy, direction and self-confidence as a Civilization. My mission is to create a positive, appreciative space in which leaders at the evolutionary edge of our Civilization can share their experience and set out their vision for our future to inspire others. They are visionaries sowing the seeds of future transformation, all genuine, creative, courageous people who care about whom we are and where we're going.

By "Civilization," I mean Western Civilization-the one I've lived in; to one that is transformed the world over the last 500 years; the one that has gone global; the one that faces enormous threats, challenges and has the unprecedented opportunity to evolve to an amazing future. When there's so much changing all at once, old structures failing and a huge array of emerging threats, that all generates a lot of anxiety, pessimism and fear which distract us from putting energy into creating new solutions, generating new ideas and envisioning a better future.

Behind the News Headlines, usually quietly, under the radar, there's a lot of good stuff going on; the seeds of the future taking root in the present. There are lots of evolutionaries trying out new ideas, new technologies, new ways of organizing and more integrated, conscious and balanced ways of thinking and being.

Western Civilization has been supremely successful in all kinds of ways of which we should be enormously proud. Science, technology, industrialization, democracy, individual rights, personal freedom, property rights, the rule of law, Christianity, humanism, organization, capitalism, feminism, civil rights, philosophy, music, art, even Imperialism have all, on balance, transformed the world for the better and have created new life conditions with new challenges and problems. In some cases, these advances had nasty side effects and some have become imbalanced. In others, they have replaced older structures and beliefs, and many babies have been lost with the bathwater.

Human Civilization is made up of human beings who are conscious beings and physical animals, all interconnected like a shoal of fish or a flock of birds. I've interviewed a huge variety of people across a variety roles, professions, beliefs, politics, status, nationalities, religions, social classes and backgrounds. What is crystal clear to me is that whilst the world we live in is hyper-complex, we operate in it using a kind of mini-map of our Civilization in our minds which we use to navigate through the world, guided by our inner compass of intuition and rational thought. It is astonishing how similar these inner maps are, and the patterns are clear. This is how we self-organize in what is a complex living system-just like a beehive or wildebeest migration.

Now we are super-connected by the internet, media and travel. We carry in our pockets access to billions of people and to just about all the knowledge that ever existed. Turning inwards we have access to instinctive intuition, heart, wisdom, common sense and judgement. Put together, that represents vast human potential and the most amazing opportunity for personal and cultural evolution ever. Looked at like that, just about all of our shared challenges and threats are solvable and a much better world is highly realistic. We're engaged in conscious evolution of ourselves and our Civilization.

There is a huge range of threats and challenges to The West and to the whole World. People focus their attention on different ones depending on their situation, beliefs and emotional make-up. The list is pretty depressing and overwhelming-so I've turned it into a list of positive questions instead. Here's a start:

- Who are we?
- Where are we going?
- What kind of future do we envisage?
- How do we rise to the challenges we face?
- What do we believe; what is right, what is wrong, what is true, what is false? What do we value and desire?
- What do we love about our Civilization?

- What works well?
- What's worth preserving and defending?
- How can we be confidently patriotic, open, diverse and global at the same time?
- How do we restore a healthy authority in ourselves, our roles and institutions?
- How can we have authority which is fair, accountable, evidence-based and respectful of complexity?
- How can be apply science effectively to complex systems like the mind, consciousness, society without oversimplification?
- How do we get sustainable, secure, clean energy?
- How do we make the welfare state to be fair to taxpayers and empowering to recipients?
- How do we balance individual rights with group responsibilities?
- Shall we start having enough children to sustain our future without depending on immigration?
- How do we absorb huge flows of immigration into a confident, open, dynamic, cohesive and secure country?
- How can we be comfortable and secure with our complex, overlapping identities?
- How do we innovate, reorganize, get our way out of recession?
- How do we enjoy the growth of human potential in harmony with the planet upon which we depend ?
- How do we evolve capitalism to serve our culture and values more holistically and fairly?
- How do we rehumanize medicine to get the best of technology whilst having compassion and healing and open our minds to the huge non-linear, non-reductionist possibilities?
- How do we refresh our democracy to deepen it rather than have occasional elections manipulated by narrow interest groups, political cabals and the media?
- Who are successful examples of organic leadership-leadership in line with human nature including self-organizing living systems, trust, respect, judgement, intuition?
- What can we learn from pioneers in consciousness and cultural evolution?
- How can we most effectively support our cultural evolution, healthy attitude to risk, judgment and responsibility?

- How do we support the evolution for a more mature, more conscious post-partisan politics which integrates left and right, individual and group, power and love, freedom and security, justice and fairness?
- How can we integrate the dark, shadow side of our history so as to unlock our power and potential?
- How do we intelligently integrate what we have come to think of as science with intuition, wisdom and complexity?
- How do we preserve and improve our open, free, democratic, pluralistic society whilst living with other cultures which actively assert their righteousness, supremacy and desire for dominance over us?
- How do we rebalance our economies to live within our means, to support the development of the emerging economies whilst remaining competitive and vibrant?
- How do we live ecologically sustainably?
- How do we have a post-postmodern spirituality which honors life and spirit and which transcends and includes existing religions and secular views?
- How do we evolve from a culture of entitlement to a culture of empowerment, maximizing potential, freedom with fairness and responsibility?
- How do we emerge beyond patriarchy and feminism to a mature, conscious masculinity and femininity, embodied, equal but different, comfortable with our inter-penetrating Yin and Yang?
- How do we re-legitimize judgement; not prejudice but healthy judgement of right and wrong, good and bad as the foundation of autonomy, freedom and authority?
- How do we get healthy hierarchies which are empowering and adaptive?
- How do we create new fields of consciousness; our energetic potential into which the future will emerge-create the field of alignment and remove the obstacles and provide the support structures and allow the self-organization to occur?
- What's already here and happening...
- What new technologies are coming which will change our way of life and opportunities?
- What are the values and beliefs of emerging new generations around the world?

- How do we foresee or create the future?
- How can we boost our cultural direction and confidence?
- Where we are fighting, what are we fighting for?
- How can we make our Civilization so attractive that others choose to align with us, emulate us and synergize with us?
- What disruptive technologies are going to change our world?
- How can we live in harmony with the planet whilst continuing to evolve our way of life?
- How can we securely and confidently live with Islam at home and abroad while it goes through its turbulent period of evolution?
- How do we ensure that the basics of food, water, clean air, energy, health and education are available fairly to everyone?
- How do we evolve wrongs of racism, nationalism, imperialism without simply inverting them to become the future victims new racisms, nationalisms and fascisms from other cultures?
- How do we deal with growing geopolitical assertiveness and military build-up by China, India, Pakistan, Russia, Iran, Brazil, Turkey, South Africa?
- Can we make use of raw materials sustainably?
- How do we stay safe with continuing nuclear proliferation to Iran, North Korea and others?
- How do we clear our massive sovereign and personal debts and live within our means?
- How can we evolve the way we do welfare, health and social care to make them affordable and more supportive of a healthy society?
- How do we enjoy the benefits of capitalism without being debt-slaves and making sure we value family, community, health, environment, education, security, freedom and human potential?
- How can we rejuvenate the family as the cornerstone of our culture?
- How do great teachers inspire, empower and carry authority in classrooms?
- How can we compete with the very determined educational competition from the East?
- How do we bring in the alienated into the mainstream with dignity and compassion?
- How do we make taxation and welfare fair for hardworking taxpayers?

- How can we eat more healthy, natural food, connected to its production whilst making it fun and practical?
- How can we farm animals in a kind, healthy way?
- How can we make care homes wonderful, heavenly places full of life, stimulation and family?
- How can hospitals empower, support and care for their staff so that they, in turn, are fit to care for their patients?
- How can we value wellbeing over objects?
- Can we revalue fatherhood and motherhood?
- Can we value life and the human spirit in a way which is inclusive of all religions, spiritualities, humanism and atheism?
- How can our organizations maximize their human potential and help their team to live their purpose and values?
- Can we restore an innocent, playful, magical childhood?
- Can we reweave community by choice or is it something we only do when we have no choice?
- Who does empowering, inspiring, visionary, values-driven, spirit-kindling leadership?
- How do we balance our budgets and trade?
- ......And so on!

# Acknowledgements

The Future of Western Civilization Series of interviews is the product of much work, many conversations and experiences over the preceding 30 years. Huge thanks to Melanie Mortiboys who has been fundamental to the project, it's conception, its incubation, birth and delivery. She has been there at every step of the way with encouragement, support, wisdom and good judgement.

The public face of the project, embodied in the series of interviews with visionary leaders got going in early 2011 with the first interview with William Nkata Masembe on the subject of patriotism from a newcomer's perspective. Many thanks to Nkata for being the first to boldly put himself on the line before the project was established.

Thank you to all those who took part in the subsequent Future of Western Civilization interviews: Melanie Mortiboys, Joseph McCormick, Martin Rutte, Dr Mary Gentile, Professor Jim Garrison, Dr Elisabet Sahtouris, Traci Fenton, Howard Bloom, Andrew Cohen, Dr Robin Wood, Chris Parish, Dr Don Beck, Herb Meyer, Neil Howe, Lynne McTaggart, Peggy Holman, Richard Barrett, Bishop Michael Nazir-Ali, Adrian Wagner, Joshua Gorman, Dr Robin Youngson, Jordan MacLeod, Mark Walsh, Soleira Green, Jim Rough, Joshua Gorman, Peter Merry, Helen Titchen Beeth, Barnaby Flynn, Danny Lambert, John Bunzl, Jon Freeman, Phil Neisser, Jacob Hess, Georgeanne Lamont, Peter Smith, Angeline Ruredzo, Steve Boley and Masana De Souza.

Behind the scenes, many people have been involved in the Future of Western Civilization project. Thanks to Linda Beecroft, Mike Beecroft, Cherie Beck, Dr Don Beck, Andrew Booth, Andrew Campbell, Chris Collins, Howard Donenfeld, Soleira Green, Samuel Humphreys, Jane MacAllister, Matthew McGuinness, Jan Mattsson, Hannah Mortiboys, Chris Parish, Martin Rutte, Lyndsey Wall, Matthew Wall, Dick Werling and Dr Robin Wood for their support and encouragement. Covers by Tatiana Villa. Formatting by Maureen Cutajar.

# Dr Nicholas Beecroft

I'm a Consultant Psychiatrist. I trained as a doctor at Guy's and St Thomas's Medical School in London, doing a BSc. in psychology at University College as part of my medical degree. After a year as a House Physician and House Surgeon, I went straight into psychiatry at the Maudsley Hospital, the Institute of Psychiatry in London where I became a member of the Royal College of Psychiatrists.

I specialize in organizational and military psychiatry and have worked with the British Army, the Royal Navy and the National Health Service.

I spent 5 years developing an interest in what I came to call "Organic Leadership," aligning organizations with human nature to unleash maximum human potential. I developed this through a combination of consulting, coaching and teaching across a wide range of organizations including McKinsey & Co., BP, Cable & Wireless, the National Health Service, British Gas and Johannesburg City Council. I helped to establish the first Department of Organizational Psychiatry outside of the USA at King's College London where I taught executives and MSc. students Organizational Psychiatry and Psychology.

I have had a lifelong interest in Foreign Policy, national identity, security and geopolitics. Whilst I was at studying at the London Business School for an MBA, I watched the September 11, 2001 terrorist attacks live on television. This and the aftermath persuaded me that it was time to transform our Foreign Policy to include the human dimension-to perceive International relations as the interrelationships between individuals, groups and mass consciousness. I set about applying the knowledge and skills from clinical psychology, psychiatry and group dynamics to diplomacy and began to consult to diplomats, politicians and journalists. I called this "Psyplomacy."

I immersed myself in Track Two (off the record) diplomacy, helping to facilitate dialogue on immigration into Europe, the Weaponization of

Space, Western-Chinese relations, European Common Foreign and Security Policy, State-building, British-German relations, Public Diplomacy, peace building, Islamic radicalization and counter-terrorism.

I worked with the Foreign & Commonwealth Office in the British Embassy in Damascus where I put the British-Syrian relationship on the psychiatrist's couch, analyzing the relationship and recommending strategies to improve it.

I influenced the British Council in London to shift their model of public diplomacy from a marketing model to a relationships-based model grounded in a clear identity, values and authentic dialogue. They launched a new policy based upon the Psyplomacy model.

After the German Foreign Minister expressed his frustration at the treatment of Germany in the British media, he accepted my proposal to work with the German Embassy in London on a psychologically informed approach to public diplomacy to improve the British German relationship.

I helped to stimulate the debate within the British government and media about Britishness, patriotism and multiculturalism which is gradually been opening up over the last 10 years. I made a substantial commitment to work behind the scenes on our strategy for the "War on Terror" which I shared in a number of places including briefing two Foreign Secretaries, the Minister for International Development, the Conservative party, the BBC, Channel 4, the Ministry of Defense and the House of Commons Foreign Affairs Select Committee.

It became clear to me that, "We" the British and, more broadly, "We" Western Civilization had lost our direction and self-confidence. I began with a series of interviews with people which I called "Britain on the Couch." The key theme across the board was a perception of loss of confidence and authority. I interviewed teachers, doctors, nurses, military personnel and the general public to find out what is the foundation of their authority? What most fascinated me was that, in spite of coming from a very broad range of backgrounds, the people spoke as one as if singing from the same hymn sheet, I could almost sense and inner compass and map which everyone shared and-there was a big wobble in it! The traditional order and self-confidence arising from clear beliefs and shared identity had been breaking down but hadn't yet been replaced by a new set of beliefs and values. Culturally we have many old baggage and maladaptive beliefs which are limiting our full potential. If we going to succeed at a time of unprecedented global change then we can and need to step up to the next level of cultural and personal evolution.

I concluded that if we are to survive and thrive in the face of the many challenges which we face then we are going to have to sort ourselves out-to be clear about who we are, where we're going, what we believe, what is right, what is wrong, what is true, what is false; to restore our self-confidence, vision and values around which we can align.

I realized that to rejuvenate our society we would need a strong spiritual foundation. That was an uncomfortable conclusion for me because I considered myself to be undeveloped in that area. I was brought up to consider Christianity and spirituality to be a naive, unscientific, superstitious and rather embarrassing relic of the past which simply wasn't necessary in the modern world. However, through my explorations I realized that we need some core foundational truths about who we are as human beings, why we're here and how we should live. So, I set about a long journey of exploration through training in Energetics, Values analysis & facilitation, Transformative-Evolutionary Coaching, Vipassana meditation, Enlightenment Intensives, Tantra, Healing, Open Space Technology and Spiral Dynamics Integral. I participated in a Circle of Trust Courage to Lead retreat, the New Warrior Training Adventure, the Mankind Project, the Culture of Honoring Initiatory Journey and have attended many workshops on improvisation and comedy. The big questions are still largely a mystery to me but I'm a bit further forward in the enquiry.

There were three main conclusions that came out of all this. One was that for all the endless negativity in the media and public conversation about the huge range of problems and threats which exist, there are a huge number of people globally working on inspirational and initiatives, ideas and visions in what is a giant process of cultural evolution throughout emerging global consciousness. As Don Beck puts it, "No more prizes for predicting the rain. Its time to build the Ark."

The second main lesson was that it is a massive waste of time and energy when we resist that which we don't like. In a fierce battle with a Marxist professor which ended in stalemate, my opponent simply collapsed and dropped away when I asked him, "if everyone took up your ideas and if the world were the way you would like it to be, what would that be like?" He simply didn't know. He'd never considered it. He only knew what he was against, what he hated. He was like a windsock with no wind. I if that to defeat all those cultural forces which I had so fiercely resisted, I simply needed to leapfrog to the other side with that incisive question. The only problem was that I couldn't answer the question myself!

The third main lesson was that we as individuals and a group have much of our power and potential locked away in our shadow, in our dark side, the wounds, the taboos, the dysfunctional beliefs, false dichotomies and the groupthink. To unlock our potential, we need to heal those wounds and shine a light on the dark side and integrate the healthy strands of all. The old false dichotomies such as left and right, male and female, love and power, freedom and control, security and openness, diversity and unity, cohesion and separation, judgement and non-judgement, truth and mystery, patriotism and globalism each have healthy and unhealthy strands which need sorting out and integrating into the whole.

In September 2011 I embarked on a project exploring the Future of Western Civilization to create a resource of interviews with visionary leaders at the evolutionary edge of our culture who can share their stories, experiences and inspirational vision is for the future. The aim is to play my part in rejuvenating the self-confidence and direction of our Civilization.

# Generational Cycles

## Predicting the Future

### Neil Howe interviewed by Dr Nicholas Beecroft

In this interview with Dr Nicholas Beecroft, Neil Howe explains the theory and sets out his observations of the current stage of the generational cycle during this "Fourth Turning" crisis period. He describes the interactions between all the various generations and predicts how the future in areas as diverse as security, immigration, family life and spiritual values. He discusses the implications for policy makers, investors and strategists as well as describing the leadership context, especially for the Boomers, Gen. X and Millennial Generations. Neil says that whilst East Asia is in synch with Western Generations, the Islamic world is slightly out of synch which has huge implications for understanding current and future geopolitics. He gives some specific consulting advice for this project, the Future of Western Civilization.

Neil Howe is a renowned authority on generations and social change in America. An acclaimed author and speaker, he is the nation's leading thinker on today's generations—who they are, what motivates them, and how they will shape America's future. Neil is founder and president of the consulting firm LifeCourse Associates, where he develops and implements cutting-edge research, analysis, and consulting services to help clients understand how generations impact marketing, workforce issues, and strategic planning.

A historian, economist, and demographer, Neil is also a recognized authority on global aging, long-term fiscal policy, and migration. He is a senior associate to the Center for Strategic and International Studies (CSIS) in Washington, D.C., where he helps direct the CSIS Global Aging Initiative.

Neil is a bestselling author who has written over a dozen books on generations, demographic change, and fiscal policy, many of them with William Strauss. Howe and Strauss' first book, Generations (1991) is a history of America told as a sequence of generational biographies. Generations, said Newsweek, is "a provocative, erudite, and engaging analysis of the rhythms of American life." Vice President Al Gore called it "the most stimulating book on American history that I have ever read" and sent a copy to every member of Congress. Newt Gingrich called it "an intellectual tour de force." Of their book, The Fourth Turning (1997), Dan Yankelovich said, "Immensely stimulating…We will never be able to think about history in the same way." The Boston Globe wrote, "If Howe and Strauss are right, they will take their place among the great American prophets."

Howe and Strauss originally coined the term "Millennial Generation" in 1991, and wrote the pioneering book on this generation, Millennials Rising, in 2000. Neil has since released several application books on Millennials—including a Recruiting Millennials Handbook for the United States Army (2001), Millennials Go To College (2003, 2007), Millennials and the Pop Culture (2005), Millennials and K-12 Schools (2008), and Millennials in the Workplace (2010). Neil work on the Millennial Generation has been featured frequently in the media, including USA Today, CNN, the New York Times, and CBS' 60 Minutes.

Previously, with Peter G. Peterson, Howe coauthored On Borrowed Time (1989; reissued 2004), a pioneering call for budgetary reform. He coauthors numerous studies for CSIS (including the Global Aging Initiative's Aging Vulnerability Index and The Graying of the Middle Kingdom: The Economics and Demographics of Retirement Policy in China). In 2008, he co-authored The Graying of the Great Powers with Richard Jackson.

**Nicholas:** Neil Howe, welcome to the series: Exploring the Future of Western Civilization.

**Neil:** Thank you. It's a pleasure to be here.

**Nicholas:** For anyone that hasn't heard of Neil's work. Neil is a Historian, an Economist and a Demographer, and he is Founding Partner and President of LifeCourse Associates. He is a global, renowned authority on generations, who they are, what motivates them, and how they'll shape our future.

He, with this wisdom, advises governments, companies and investors. He's written many books including *Generations*, the *13th Generation, Generation X*, and it was he and his partner that originally coined the term: the *Millennial Generation* with their book, *Millennials Rising*.

I, personally, came to know of Neil when I read *The Fourth Turning*, which comes out of an amazing piece of scholarly study of generations going back through America and then back into Britain, for about 400 years, where they spotted the patterns of how generations cycle, and what we experience in our own brief period and believe is unique, is actually something that's repeated many times in different forms over history.

I was blown away when I read that book, because I think it was published in 1997, but it's written as if it were written now, with a full knowledge of September 11th, and subsequent events, and also the economic crisis that we are in, it's absolutely remarkable.

Neil, I'm really delighted that you were able to join me, and I'd like to focus on your predictions, vision, and advice regarding the Future of Western Civilization.

To kick off, obviously some people won't have come across your generations' theory, and they won't have read your books. I wonder if, so that people can follow the conversation that follows, if you could say a little bit of an introduction about the theory of generations and, in particular focus on the *Fourth Turning*.

**Neil:** Yes. I think the best way is to say something about how I got into this subject. This is in late 1980s, I and another writer, William Strauss, wanted to write something about generational differences, throughout our history and we were both baby Boomers, classic. We always thought generations mattered, and we wanted to explore this subject, and it turned out to be a huge project, which ultimately resulted in our first book, for which we got a generous advance to write, otherwise we couldn't have taken three years of our lives to delve back into history and to do all this.

That was published in 1991, that was the book called *Generations, the History of America's Future*, and it basically looked at all generations in

American history going back to the early 17th Century, the immigrants from the Old World. In that book we found that we told the history of America the way it's never been told before. In fact, history itself has never been told as a sequence of generational biographies.

Remember when people when talked about history, they talk about what people of any one age bracket is doing one year after the next, year after the next. It's typically midlife leaders and parents, this is what they did this year, this is what they did the next year and so forth. Occasionally, the history of childhood or youth where you'd find out what 13 year olds are doing one year to the next, but they never track the same people over time, right.

We thought, let's write our history completely differently. For the first time let's start with a group of people who have a certain location in history, raised these kids at a certain time, and follow their story throughout the rest of their lives, this is what one of the great generations thinkers of the Nineteenth Century has once likened generations to tiles on a roof. They go like this because if you plot age on one axis and time on the other, generations are diagonal, so they're like tiles on a roof, and that's what we did.

We found even neighboring generations experience many of the same events that they experienced when they're different ages, and one generation takes part in a war, the next generation were children doing the war, right, that kind of thing. We did that for each generation, looking out at how they're raised, how they come of age, youth, courtship. How they behave as midlife adults and leaders, and old age. How they look back at what they've done and the younger people are doing, and what we found is that even neighboring generations look at the world completely differently, and this is not new.

This is not something, today with Generation X versus Boomers, this goes back to the Founding Fathers, it goes back to the 17th Century, generational tension. Not only do we find generations are very different, we found that these differences, now this is the most exciting discovery, these differences have occurred in a certain pattern, so that certain kinds of generations always followed other kinds of generations.

This is important because generations are shaped by history, and then shape history, so if there's a pattern in generations there's a pattern in history itself.

This is discovery toward the end of the generations that we introduce, but it's something that we explored much more fully in the book, that you cited in 1997, *The Fourth Turning*, where we really start with the whole idea of cyclicality in history. Why and why are rhythms in history, and how do generations explain those rhythms? You know, we all know when people study social sciences, at least those who, like to think in visionary ways about how it all works. We all come across these cyclical theories: in American history, cycles of realigning elections, for example, is very familiar to people. Cycles of family life, cycles in drug use, cycles in the economy, the K-waves, the Kondratiev waves, the long cycle in the economy, which many people obviously are talking about now, given what's happening in the economy. Cycles of demography, cycles in immigration, and so forth, but we've thought that are these rhythms, and they are explained by a governing cycle, a sort of an underlying cycle which is driven by generational aging. This is the one biological and social fact about the human life which gives a periodicity to these three cycles. If we have a cycle as war and peace, why isn't it three years, why isn't it 300 years? It's the certain length of time because we all grow up and grow old in a certain pattern; right?

**Nicholas:** Yes.

**Neil:** That gave rise to the idea of turnings. Now, a generation is a group of people born over a period around 20 years or so, and the length is about the length of the phase life; between being born and coming of age fully as an adult. Similarly, these turnings which are these eras of history, these certain social moods that we experience for a period of time, are also about the same length of time. During each turning, a new generation is entering in childhood and another generation is coming of age in the young adults, and another generation is retiring, and so each turning is attuned to the sequence of each generation moving into the next phase of life.

We saw that there was a correspondence between generations and turnings, and that it was very important in governing our history, and why history feels so differently to us, often from one decade to the next, and why it feels so differently for new generations coming in, in a different turning.

Now, we discovered a cycle of four turnings and each of these corresponds with the coming of age of a different kind of generation. The First Turning, we call a high, this is typically a period that occurs right after a great crisis, but during these periods, institutions are strong, individualism is weak, society feels a strong consensus about where everyone wants to go, there's a great sense of progress, it's how it feels like we are more than the sum of our parts. We are greater than we are as individuals, and also when minorities are shunted to the side, that Vernon Parrington once called these *the great barbecues of American history*. We just sit around and enjoy who we are and think about the future a lot, the Second Turning...

**Nicholas:** In our cycle that was the 1950s?

**Neil:** Yes. The term *"the American high"* comes from William O'Neil, an American historian, to correspond basically with the presidencies of Truman and Eisenhower and John Kennedy, as a period. This would have also been the period of the Post Civil War, Victorian high of Industrialization and nation-building; the Post Revolutionary Era of Good Feelings, the Virginia Presidencies of Madison and Monroe and so on.

The Second Turning is what we call "an *awakening*, and these have occurred repeatedly through, not only American history, but much of European history as well. This is a period where suddenly everyone wants to throw off all the social obligation, all the conformity, all the group thing, everyone wants to re-find themselves again, what's going on in here? We want some sense of personal authenticity.

We date the most recent awakening as, sort of, loosely the Consciousness Revolution, that period that it started at least in the United States from the mid-1960s, went all the way through into, maybe, the early 1980s. It started with revolts on college campuses, mainly in the form of cultural protests, and finally ended with deregulation and tax revolts, and the whole theme was, "Leave me alone. Don't tell me to do anything I don't want to do," and it ran the gamut really.

17

Some Boomers who were occupying their campuses, and turning their fraternities and the communes back in the mid-'60s, all the way through those, many of those same Boomers are who ended up voting for Ronald Reagan. Cutting taxes, and becoming yuppies, and a much more individualized view of American lives, and how we negotiate.

Robert Putnam, the famous Harvard Sociologist, wrote a book not long ago, *Bowling Alone*. He asked the question why do Americans bowl alone today? We used to go to the Elks Club; used to go with the Chamber of Commerce, now we just go alone when we want to go bowling. Why this change? He examined every single variable: women in the workplace, television, everything. He said, "Two-thirds of it is just generational replacement."

There's new people aging into these phases of life, are doing things alone that the older generation used to do as groups, generational replacement. I mean, think of Boomers, this is the first generation of women who expect to be economically independent. This is historically unprecedented. We forget how revolutionary that awakening was at reshaping our expectations.

That was the awakening and many historians will call this consciousness revolution, America's fourth or fifth great awakening, and the sequence that goes back, either to John Winthrop in the 1630s, or Jonathan Edwards in the 1740s, and in the long history of awakenings in America, this is one of them.

**Nicholas:** Now you're going to come to the depressing bit, which is the bit that I…

**Neil:** That's when you came along! (both laughing)

**Nicholas:** That's when I was born, yes.

**Neil:** That's right. I've often said that there was something in Generation X similar to the psychology of divorce. The child always thinks, "My parents were happy until I came along; it must be my fault," right? That's the thing with Generation X collectively, there is this psychology of, you know, everything was fine in society, in history, until we came along as a group, and then everyone started arguing, that nothing works anymore.

The Third Turning which follows an awakening is mainly the opposite of a high. Institutions are distrusted and discredited, individualism is strong and flourishing, and I will say, in many ways, and still are a little bit in a Third-Turning mentality, where over the last two-and-a-half decades, at least, you walk into a bookstore, the most upbeat books in a bookstore about *me, myself, and I*, right. How I'm going to conquer, because I can do anything. Anything you read, any book title about what we do collectively, is depressing. It's like the end of politics, the end of society, the end of family. That's how we think, that's the Third Turning.

**Nicholas:** Yes; the decay of all the old structures.

**Neil:** The decay of the structures, and in a way though, it feels liberating because it's in a way, during a high, we are learning the lessons of the recent crisis, which is you've got to band together to be strong, so we unlock that formula, building lots of infrastructure and doing all that stuff. In awakening we learn the lesson: No, no, you need to atomize, be yourselves, and in a way the subsequent Third Turning is living with that approach.

We are all kind of happy pursuing our own individual lives. Well, history suggests that Third Turnings are nearly always followed by a Fourth Turning, and this is a period where, often, it occurs as a crisis or a period of very palpable urgency in history when we are forced to rebuild institutions again. The Second Turning is all about rebuilding our inner world; it's all about values and morality and culture, and sort of inner priorities. The Fourth Turning is all about the outer world. It's all about the economy, politics, empire, and it's about outer world institutions.

If an historical event doesn't trigger a Fourth Turning, a Fourth Turning leader might even invent a crisis in order to galvanize collection action. It gives a culture which lost its purpose in the Third Turning, a purpose again, often in the form of propaganda. During the 1930s, and particularly during World War II, all the Hollywood stars were brought to Washington to produce propaganda. That's how we gave the culture a purpose again. We had very particular objects we had to attain to survive, and also, and of course during it, we all begin to re-find ourselves as members of groups again, members of communities.

The 1930s, which is our last Fourth Turning; it's often called The Decade of Belonging. There are many a stories we read about that period. After the 1920s which was a very wild and sort of an edgy period, this is the great period of regionalism in short story fiction, for example, and then we began to write about every little place. What's unique about it, how did everyone get along together during the Depression? One important effect of the *New Deal* was getting people to form associations again, and group together, even cartelize the economy so that we would no longer be competing anymore on price.

**Nicholas:** Well I experienced that personally without knowing it, without knowing your structure. Growing up in the Third Turning, of things decaying, everything falling apart; everyone moaning that everything was worse than it used to be, no longer having the ideal that science would solve everything. Yet, with my grandparents' generation saying that: we used to be poor, and we had to fight the Second World War, but we loved it, and it was the happiest time of our lives. Everyone was together, and united, and there was a great sense of belonging, and it's all been downhill ever since, and so yes. What's great, actually wonderful about your theory is, is to put it in the big, historical context and say, "That's a cycling pattern and not just our own micro-environment."

That brings me to the question. Are we now in the Fourth Turning, and specifically, I suspect that September the 11th, when that happened, was in the Third Turning, wasn't it, because we haven't had a Fourth Turning response to that?

**Neil:** Yes. It was. I would say that George W. Bush, at least in his foreign policy, tried to become a Fourth Turning President, but the time wasn't right for that. I think you could say. The timing was not right. We have a lot of readers who told us that, "Gee, 9/11, that's a Fourth Turning, right?" Even at the time we consistently said, "no," because none of the generations were old enough.

There's a certain pattern that has to occur. Each generation has to be moving into its next phase of life. That was not yet happening. We never predicted anything as early as 2001. Boomers weren't yet retiring, the Millennial Generation wasn't yet really in college, Gen Xers weren't really quite entering midlife yet. Later in the decade, yes, and tentatively what I date as the beginning of the Fourth Turning is with 2008: the global financial meltdown, and a very interesting, extraordinary election in America in 2008, too, with the election of the first African-American President, Barack Obama.

At least two things happened at the same time, but particularly, the meltdown which is now having further repercussions around the world. I think everyone agrees that this severe recession which the entire developed world experienced, is not your typical demand recession. It's a deleveraging recession. You look at the works of Rogoff and Reinhart, and many others, and you realize, this is going to take years to unravel. This is going take years to deleverage the economy.

In the meantime we are suddenly in the midst of that, having to face all of the other issues of unfunded liabilities for all these entitlements that we all put off, and now we have to deal at the worst of all possible times. Economically, I see this very difficult scenario in which, at least in the United States, we are running very large deficits, and we either have to basically pull down the deficits, and basically slow down economic stimulus at a time when our economy is still very vulnerable. Or, let our debt to GDP ratio, drift up into the real danger zone.

Net debt to GDP of maybe 90 percent or more by the end of this decade, and this is a very unpleasant choice. In the meantime, we've got all these larger problems, about healthcare and aging costs. I think one area, too, and looking at this globally, sort of global Fourth Turning, you have many of these same general occurrence in Europe. I met some film teams over from the Netherlands. They happen to come over to the United States, and they happen to interview me; about the Obama generation, or about this generation, or that generation. They just think that in America that's where all the generational things are happening, right?

**Nicholas:** Right.

**Neil:** The last time they came over I said, "Why don't you guys do something on Generational change in Europe. You realize this is going on in Europe now." It's a complete shift. All the new leaders don't remember World War II. Europe, the whole European Unity project was run by a generation that had either fought in World War II, or had experienced it in the children.

These are the dutiful builders and, above all, they wanted peace. Peace, the horrors of the war that they remember as children. Well they're passing from the scene now, and if you look at what the Germans think of Greek citizens, and what the Greeks think of the French, and French think of the Italians, we are in a new generational territory, and I think in Europe there's a particularly volatile situation because the political institutions are obviously much weaker.

They're much more recent, they've really never been tested before, and then the political economic challenges you face with aging, and with their own time and structure, to tell you the truth, much vaster than our own in the United States. Not actually so much in the U.K., but particularly on the Continent, particularly the Mediterranean countries: Portugal, Spain, Italy and so on down the line, where there's no easy out there, and this has repercussions because it comes back to America.

The big question in America now in 2012 is: well, our own economy seems to be gaining speed, but basically it's either; will Iran, or in Europe, basically derail us and shove us back into a recession again. That's the question and I think, again, that's a little bit of the turnings working through and around other areas of the world.

**Nicholas:** Thank you. Thank you for that, Neil, that's great. You've already mentioned a bit about how, obviously, Europe is pretty much in synch with the American cycles. I've read it in your book that you thought that some of the Asian countries are as well. That's quite obvious in Japan and even in China. I'm wondering about the Islamic world, because you mentioned that Europe is in a dodgy state, really, and of course we are right next to North Africa and the Middle East. I don't know what cycle they're in, but they're bursting with young people. Something like, three-quarters of the population under 25.

22

They are full of energy, they are having very large families, very large numbers of them are coming across to Europe, particularly France and Italy and Holland, but many of the countries, many European cities. Also, the belief systems which they hold, although they might be changing quite fast, and hopefully, becoming democratic and pluralistic as quickly as possible, but nevertheless, there's quite strong strands of authoritarian, patriarchal and, sort of, intolerant, absolutistic belief systems, and with a spiritual foundation in Islam at a time when, of course, in Europe most of us have completely give up on those things, moving into being sensitive, liberal, humanistic, relativistic.

**Neil:** Right.

**Nicholas:** Anyway, you get the point. With your theory of generations, what happens when you put those two together?

**Neil:** Let me address that, and say a few contrarian things here.

**Nicholas:** Okay.

**Neil:** First of all let me address this demographic part, because I'm a demographer, and actually I help head up the Global Aging Initiative, with CSIS, the Center for Strategic and International Studies down here in D.C. One thing that people are unaware of is that there's a huge deceleration in fertility, not just in the developed world, but in the developing world. This has hugely affected Latin America, which now, since the early 1980s and particularly the late 1980s and 1990s, has a fertility rate is not too much higher than ours, in the United States.

Combine that with the recent recession, we have had, almost no one knows this, we've had almost a complete drying up of immigration in the last few years.

**Nicholas:** Really?

**Neil:** This last year immigration from Mexico was almost to zero, almost zero. The immigration authorities, are suddenly doing almost nothing along the border of Mexico right now. I'm looking at the demography of Latin

America; I don't think we will ever experience the kind of migration that we experienced in the 1990s. I don't think it's coming back. I just don't see it. Families that used to have six kids are now having two.

**Nicholas:** Plus those who can will be going to Brazil instead.

**Neil:** People are unaware that Iran has experienced probably the most dramatic fertility decline of any generation in the Twentieth Century; from six children per woman, right at the time of the Iranian Revolution of the late '70s, early '80s, when they were fighting Iraq. Now it's down to something like 1.6, they are under-replacement right now.

**Nicholas:** Yes.

**Neil:** So you have this enormous youth-wave with very few kids coming by. It creates a set of waves actually, it's almost turbulence that occurs.

Let me speak now to this generational part of it. The Islamic world is a little bit different, and I'm talking about North Africa, and the Arab world and Iran, and to some extent Turkey and the Turkic Republics; so that whole area. They are on slightly different schedules; we think that in terms of turnings in generations, they're almost a generation behind where we are in the United States. It's very interesting to think that a lot of the Fourth Turning events which, for us, occurred in the '30s and early '40s, for them occurred in the '50s, early '60s, because that's when a lot of these countries were being founded, the new republics were being created, the Baath Party, for example, which was set up by strong, Pan Arab, a very secular Baathist young men and Generals, who has set up a lot of these regimes in Iraq and Egypt and so on. This was more their Fourth Turning which is a little bit later than ours. Then what happened was, is that you had the kids who were born just after that creation, the classic prophet archetype. These are the kids coming along just after the business and civic institutions are put into place. That's your prophet archetype.

These were born, really starting in the late 1950s through the '60s and so, when we were having Generation X, they were having a prophet archetype, and when you look at Osama Bin Laden, or Mahmoud Ahmadinejad, or you look at the leader in Lebanon, Nasrallah, you look at all of these guys, you look at the leader of the Taliban in Afghanistan, all these guys were born in late 1950.

They were all born in Iran 1957-'58, and many of them had the experience of growing in a very secular order, which they wanted protest against. There is something almost Shakespearean about Osama Bin Laden, right, because what did his father do? We have these late Boomers had these G.I. parents that rebuilt the Interstate, and rockets to the moon and all this happening.

Of course, they're always arguing, "What's the moral purpose of all you're building? What did Osama Bill Laden's father do? He did nothing but construct billions of tons of marble and concrete for this new Saudi regime. That's all he did was build.

**Nicholas:** So he's the equivalent of an American campus, sort of, Woodstock person?

**Neil:** Well, yes. Here's something very interesting that people don't know about, but when people think of Islamic Awakening, we even use word, right, the *Islamic Awakening*. It basically started in 1979, and not in the mid-'60s, almost the turning later. The epicenter for that was 1979, it was the Iran Revolution, it was the Soviet invasion of Afghanistan fighting the Mujahideen. It was the attack on Mecca, a couple of the terrorists, took over Mecca for a week. It's one of the things that was often not talked about, but Saudi Arabia really controlled it, and then you had, not long after that, the assassination of Anwar Sadat.

Now that was the beginning of this whole new awareness, not just an occasional hijacking of a plane, or doing something weird, but suddenly a whole new generation was feeling different about what ought to be done, and this group, throughout the '80s and '90s, is now beginning to age. They are now the age of the Islamic Brotherhood, they are the midlife generation.

The generation coming after them is more your Nomadic X-ers, and it's very interesting to you look in Iran or Egypt, these kids don't want to band together and build these things, they just want to get ahead and get out, and if they can get out they would, but they basically are very much interested just in their own lives. We predicted, when the Arab Spring came about, given the generations in charge, that the young adults, being the basic Nomad generation, they were going to be powerless politically, they were not, themselves, going to impress their will on the new political institutions.

Rather it was the Brotherhood which actually had built institutions, social service organizations which now we see. Now they're dominating the new parliamentary institutions in Egypt, and I think the real thing to watch for in the Arab world, and as well as in the Iranian circuit, is what will happen between that generation of the students that took over the embassy and the brotherhood which is now in midlife, and the generation coming after these Xers; the generation now just beginning to enter their teens; that's the new hero archetype.

Those are the two that historically have had the extremely strong and effective, powerful historical relationship. The real implication, the real repercussions of this won't be felt for a while. I think that the Middle East remains an extremely unstable area, anything can happen.

**Nicholas:** Certainly, so you're saying that in that region the people who are currently just coming into their teens; they are the Nomad Generation, and they will get together ...

**Neil:** The kids who were just starting to get into their teens, this is actually the cutting edge of a new hero Generation.

**Nicholas:** Oh, right.

**Neil:** The people in their late teens, and 20s, and all of that, they are basically the Nomad archetype, they are the nomads, they are the survivors, they just want their own lives to work. They want more freedom, this kind of generation has only wanted more freedom to do the things they have to do, and you see this very strongly in Iran, for example, where you see the young people, they haven't been very effective as a political force, but they are certainly a very libertarian, pro-market, *don't*

26

*tread on me* kind of generation. They are not certainly going to be organizing an alternative, but they're certainly very hostile to the very strongly, idealistic and values-oriented types, the peers of Ahmadinejad, people in their 50s and 60s who themselves are different from the Ayatollah, actually somewhat secular.

People have to realize that Mahmoud Ahmadinejad and his peers are not really the oldest generation operative in Iran, they are the ones who have been taking over, they hay have not even reached their zenith in power yet. You have many other generations in play. I think it's similar in much of Asia, I mean, if we got the average Asian, and the leadership of India and Bangladesh and so on, these are very often people in their 70s, right, very typical leaders, are actually quite old by our standards, and in China as well.

**Nicholas:** Hmm? That's absolutely fascinating. Can you see ahead to, say, 15 years time when the Islamic world has a Fourth Turning by your prediction? Are there any idea this far ahead what that might look like?

**Neil:** I have no idea, but we expect that the danger is likely to be much more conventional than disorder. In other words, it is going to be a power which actually can cohesively focus its collective energy on something rather than shattered groups and failed states, you know, fragments of this and that is what we worry about today.

From the generational perspectives of other awakenings throughout history, other violent awakenings; the Protestant Reformation, for example, which was incredibly violent; gave rise to wars all over Europe. The sequence matters. How did it look differently to the generation that comes of age in it, the generation that was already adult when it broke out, the generation of children during it, and the generation born after it?

In other words, how does it look to generations with different locations relative to that event; and we think that if you looked at that, you could probably establish incredibly important patterns which would actually give an insight into where things are going.

**Nicholas:** What happens when people, immigrants move from one country to another, where say, if someone came from Algeria to France, so if the generational cycles were out of synch, do they quickly adapt and catch up with the new country, or do they sit in parallel for a while?

**Neil:** I think they adapt, normally. That has been the American experience maybe a little bit different in that in Europe where immigrants don't assimilate as much. You think of all the Turks living in Germany, who still have the satellite dishes, to get them political news from Turkey, right, they're still, practically, in Turkey even though they live in Germany. I mean, obviously that's a different kind of situation. I think also though, it's important to remember that that migration itself has its turning dimension.

That is to say, assuming that in American history, it's been true, that Third Turnings have been our high immigrant periods, because these are periods when institutions being weak, borders are weak, and we don't mind having a lot of new people on our hands, why not, right?

**Nicholas:** Right.

**Neil:** Whereas our Fourth and First Turnings tend to be much more restrictive.

**Nicholas:** I see.

**Neil:** Now the least immigrant generations in American history, a smaller share of immigrants as a share of the population, it's the Silent Generation. Americans born in the late '20s, '30s, early '40s, not many people were immigrating to America, during World War Two. Typically people migrated as young adults, not many people were migrating to America in the '40s and '50s, and it wasn't all that attractive during the war, and also it was very restricted.

We hugely opened up immigration laws in 1965, and then even more, so Boomers in America are the generation of rising immigration, and Generation X in the United States is the generation with the highest share of immigrants per capita, of any generation going all the way back to the Lost Generation, who were in the 1880s and 1890s.

**Nicholas:** Obviously, we are all interconnected, but coming back for the time being to Western Civilization, we are in a Fourth Turning, we are at the beginning phase of that, and you listed many ways in which we are just about to drive off a cliff. At this stage, from your research, and your experience, is there anything we can do to affect the outcome, to effect a positive outcome, or once that gets going, does it just take on a nature of its own that you can't really stop?

**Neil:** I think you can be helpful, but you can be helpful in the context of understanding what's possible, given the turning you're in, or even given where you are in the turning. I know in policy circles, and I'm here in Washington, D.C., there are a lot of people that were inventing reforms. We are going to reform the lobbying system, we are going to reform social security and medicare, reforms, and they are completely divorced from any sense of what's possible now. What's the mood? What can be done, right?

**Nicholas:** Yes.

**Neil:** I often tell people, I tell reformers, my advice to them is strange, that you get your reform all in order, you know, get it ready, but just put it on the shelves for now, because there will be a moment when suddenly, in an hour of urgency, there's going to be a number of politicians in a dark room and, I don't know, the DOW is going to be down 1500 points, right. The dollar is going to be … you get my drift, right?

**Nicholas:** Yes.

**Neil:** Basically it's what happened in late September 2008, when Ben Bernanke and others came to Congress, met with Pelosi. Ben Bernanke said, "It's time to break the glass." He said, "You pass this legislation by Friday or we might not have an economy by Monday." We know that this was now said in closed sessions, in a real mood, I don't know if you recall. That was free fall, and finally even the money markets were freezing up. You literally didn't know what was going to happen next day.

That's the mood we are talking about, so in that mood, people are going to be looking around and they are going to be saying, we not only needed something big, we need to implement it in four hours, and that will be the urgency. We forget that history is not continuous, history is

29

discontinuous. It's like the seasons that way. There are times in our history when nothing seems to change publicly. I mean in the 1990s, what happened in public life in America of any lasting importance. I mean, it's hard to point to anything. I don't know, it's O.J. Simpson, and Monica Lewinsky, we had this, we had that. What did we really do in that decade? Consider the late 1930s and early 1940s, consider 1936 to '46, you know, coming out of World War II, invented Bretton Woods, the U.N., the World Bank, the IMF, you just go down all these, the Marshall Plan, you look around there were great men doing huge promethean things; suddenly, all within a certain timespan.

Why does history suddenly speed up like that, and then we slow down like that? Well, we think turnings explain that, and what we think is that when you get toward the climax of a Fourth Turning, suddenly you're going to have to implement all these things.

It's interesting, in the 1920s, people did lots of work on Pension Reform, a lot of scholars did work, no one listened to it, ignored completely the ivory towers, but then in 1934, Roosevelt appointed, at a very dark hour for America, the Committee on Economic Security, and months later they developed this enormous piece of legislation called the Social Security Act, which gave rise to, all of our means-tested programs such as the Social Security Security Act, they set up the whole framework of the New Deal and the Welfare State was in that one piece of legislation, and suddenly all those academics, who have been toiling, in obscurity, were suddenly called to Washington to get their blueprint, because we need it, it's going into effect, you know, right now.

**Nicholas:** That's quite optimistic really, is saying: although there is a deterministic streak, and we are all part of this mass process, you're saying, now definitely prepare, envision the future, come up with solutions, but don't expect them to happen immediately, they'll happen when the time is right.

**Neil:** Yes.

**Nicholas:** That's very positive. I was born in what you called the Generation X, so born in 1970 and so I totally resonate with what was in your book of growing up in the era when people talked about the Golden Age and the past, and everything was falling apart, and all the old structures being challenged and so on.

Even though I really enjoyed your book, because it's fascinating, from a personal perspective, it was depressing because it seems like history skips over the nomad generation.

**Neil:** The nomad, yes.

**Nicholas:** What is my generation's role, if any? Do we just have to get out the way and mind our own business? What's our role in this Fourth Turning?

**Neil:** Maybe you got so depressed you didn't read the last chapter, because in the last chapter, the 13th Gen, we talked exactly to that. What is the destiny of your archetype? What do you do historically that matters? What we've basically said was, is it during your years of prying, public influence? When the Nomad Archetype is in midlife, that's when they make or break it, they save the world.

Typically these generations started young, left to their own devices to develop this pragmatic, well travelled, resourceful, resilient persona that we all associate with your generation; suddenly those qualities are embodied in the midlife leaders at the heart and climax of the Fourth Turning, when everyone depends upon those leaders to get it right. Now you will have older Prophet Archetypes, and they'll be giving all the eloquent sermons. They'll be doing their vision thing, but they will not be the older leaders, elder leaders. They will not be the main group of leaders actually controlling how things are playing out on the ground, so to speak.

Then you will have the younger millennials, those will be your guys, they will be optimistic, they'll be very powerful and cohesive with all of their teamwork, and they will be all together on Facebook and social media, and they'll be doing huge things that you're going to try to harness, but they'll be looking up to your generation for leadership.

**Nicholas:** Right.

**Neil:** All of history, in a sense, and that's the timing of history, that all of public history, depends upon the generation that was thrown away, right, your generation, the nomads?

**Nicholas:** Right.

**Neil:** We saw this, for example, in World War II. When you look at the generation of Eisenhower, and George Patton, and Omar Bradley, and all of that group; that were the dauntless leaders; that took us through World War II. They were from the Lost Generation. I mean, that was the generation that was the throw-away generation of 1900. The kids that no one cared about, and many of them led a life of individualism and entrepreneurship, people forget that Harry Truman tried to set up businesses several times. They all went bust. He had no real money, finally got caught in the political machine, he was chosen by FDR as an afterthought, and he suddenly became President. He took us through the A-bomb, the building of the H-bomb, the Korean War, all of that, and when he retired he still had no money, he was begging France. Now we hadn't any pensions yet, for ex-Presidents, we did that later with Kennedy, but here was this guy, just thrown into it all.

Truman's attitude toward himself, was one of complete self-deprecation, I mean, I don't expect anything from it. Another character in American history, very similar, was that of John Adams. Another Nomad Archetype who coped with America at the heart of the crisis, and had horrible self esteem. I can't write, I can't think the times are too tough, maybe we need a monarchy after all; one way or another he got: this is the generation that got America through the crisis, and it's actually fascinating to look at that, within the context of the founding of America.

During the Constitutional Convention, all of the political leaders that were pushing for stronger centralized control, the Madisons and Hamiltons and Jeffersons, and all, they were all younger leaders, they were the Republican Generation. You know that archetype because the Patrick Henrys, they were saying: leave us alone, we don't want that, but they got it, and then they made it work.

You can imagine today it's the same thing. When we have our big solution come the year 2020 or 2022 or whenever it happens, you can imagine

X'ers saying, "No, we don't want this, you government. No, we don't want it, but if we had to have it, let's make it right." I mean, that's same pragmatic attitude, but on the other hand, let's make it right, let's make it work. We see that again and again through history. I think your generation is the generation that everyone will have to count on. It's interesting that there are only two countries in the developed world who have yet, Nomad Archetype leaders.

One is United States with Barack Obama, born in 1961, pure Generation X. New Age mom, family broke up, sort of divorce, complete disorientation of his childhood, and now Barack Obama goes around and talks of himself as a post-boomer leader. I mean, that's in his autobiography, he talks about it all the time; and in Britain. You have a new leader of your own generation, right?

**Nicholas:** Yes. David Cameron.

**Neil:** It's interesting. You have two examples of the new styles beginning to take. It's just now the opening in a way, and you should see more of that as time goes on.

**Nicholas:** Yes. Although, of course, in both cases the rest of the population aren't yet ready to get along with them.

**Neil:** No.

**Nicholas:** I mean, to make it really personal, this project that I'm doing, *Exploring the Future of the Western Civilization*, to put it in the language of your book, it's to navigate us through the Fourth Turning, to try to download the wisdom of your generation, of the Boomer generation, all these great ideas, and download them in a way that's practical, that can then inspire what you call the Millennial Generation to actually enact it, and do it.

**Neil:** Correct.

**Nicholas:** That's the purpose. I suppose, two questions embedded in that. One is looking at what I've done so far, the majority of the people

33

I've spoken to are of the Boomer Generation. That's great, because there's a hell of a lot of wisdom and knowledge and....

**Neil:** Also we love to talk, right?

**Nicholas:** Yes.

**Neil:** We love to talk.

**Nicholas:** I definitely recognize what you talk about, the vision but not necessarily the walking the talk, or the follow through. I definitely, personally witnessed that, but should there come a point where my generation says: thanks, very much and cut off and stop listening, and push you away, or do we keep you on our shoulder and have you as wise elders that are guiding us?

**Neil:** Well, let's hope the wise elders' role works. That is the ideal role, and I think one of the insights looking at history, in terms of turnings in generations is to not expect each generation to behave the same way. I think it's the same thing, at the workplace, I do a lot of consulting with generations in the workplace, we have diagnostic survey tools, to go in and actually look at generational points, and the problem is that the Boomer, supervisor and manager thinks these Xers should be just like he was at age 40, and these Millennials should be just like he was at age 20.

Rather than thinking: no, they're never going to be like me, they're fundamentally different. How can I take advantage of their strengths? Do you see what I mean? Completely different perspective, how can I acknowledge their differences and then take advantage of that division of labor? Completely a different way of looking at it, and I think the same thing when we are thinking of how the different generations are going to get along in the Fourth Turning.

The idea is not so much to say, we don't want you to be as much as like the generation as you are but rather: how can we put your talent to best use. You Boomers, you're great at this, why don't you focus on that, and let us focus on what we are doing, and then...

**Nicholas:** What about in the other direction? I'm in a phase of down-loading and distilling the wisdom, if you like, so I'm happy with what I've done so far, but in looking at the Google analytics of who actually looks at the videos, the interviews, it's mostly age 35 to 65, and few of the generation younger than me, the sort of Millennials, have looked at all.

What, going forward, once I finish the current phase, what's going to be required to engage them, both to get them interested to be relevant to them, and to really harness their energy for the benefit of the big picture, of rejuvenating the self confidence and direction of Western Civilization?

**Neil:** Well, I could give you some advice on that. I think what you need to do is take your curriculum, chop it up and make it bite-size. Give them feedback at every stage along the way when they're reading, and then have an organized task that they can get through. Have a completion point; give them the goals. Let them put them put it on their résumé, and let them use that as credentials that they can then take. I mean, think about millennial now, you've got a much more conventional, organized mindset.

**Nicholas:** Sure.

**Neil:** It's, how is this going to be useful in their lives? It's not that they're not interested in it, but they want to know how they can make it useful as the step to go on and build, and it's obvious how you would make the case. They would say, "You need to know these paradigms, right." Wherever you go, you need to know these paradigms, whatever you're building, whatever cornerstone that you're working on, and to put in place, you need to be aware of this, but you need to boil its pur-pose down, so they understand what it is. It's this kind of Revision notes to Boomer Wisdom you've got here.

**Nicholas:** There's one thing I didn't quite understand. I thought that it was meant to be my generation who were the individualists who didn't cooperate. I thought the Millennial Generation were more civic-minded and group orientated.

**Neil:** They are, they are, but they have certain things in common with Xers, any two neighboring generations usually have something in common and something that they differ. It's the second gen ... it's the generation at the opposite ends of the sequence before that it's truly opposite. The generation that you're truly opposite from would be the Silent Generation, or the generation coming along after the Millennials, right?

**Nicholas:** Right.

**Neil:** They are little toddlers today, but the Millennials, yes, they are into things that you're not into, they are constructive, they are positive, they are into teamwork, they trust the institutions, a lot of that stuff. Now, your generation does not, but they do insist that things be made practical. To make it digestible and attractive to Millennials, they need to know the purpose. They're not just going to go and just mess around in it for a while. That's the Boomer thing. I'm just going to expand my mind for a few hours.

One hour, they're busy, their schedule, they're planners, so you need to say, "You do this 15 minutes a day, or 20 minutes a day, here's the program, check it off as you go along. You get to the end. You have the credential, and you can then use it socially, right, and constructively to say, "This is my credential and it fits in with your project which is that." Do you see what I mean?

**Nicholas:** I see. That's fascinating and I'm really pleased I asked you.

**Neil:** You've got to make it into a square thing that they can fit somewhere.

**Nicholas:** I would never have guessed that, and that, unfortunately, is not my personality so that's a real challenge to....

**Neil:** Then each generation has to adjust to the needs of other generations.

**Nicholas:** Yes, that's quite a challenge. What's going to happen to security in the next generation?

**Neil:** I think security will be an issue. It's all going to rise as part of the frame of what national security threats we perceive to be abroad, and then we saw what happened after 9/11. Interestingly; and there's a Fourth Turning aspect to it, the enormous national security apparatus that was set up, the Patriot Act, and everything else in Washington, D.C., has not atrophied at all. It's just as big as it ever was, and it's now sitting there all over the world. We now have Predators, flying the world around with pilotless planes, not far from here in Virginia, they are sitting here with their joysticks, flying these things over, Yemen and Somalia, you know.

**Nicholas:** From what you just said, it sounds like the Millennials won't kick against that, they'll be happy to be put in a box.

**Neil:** Yes. I think they will once it's demonstrated as a problem. Don't forget that the Millennial Generation in America, by two-thirds to one-third voted for the Democratic Party, voted for Obama, was not in favor of the intervention in Iraq, and wants to cooperate with other countries more than they perceive the Americans doing. On the other hand, I find this interesting; they are also one of the most optimistic generations about the future, as they still think that Iraq will come out fine, that Afghanistan will come out fine. They are not negative, they're not pessimistic like a lot of Xers, they actually think, despite everything that we've done, everything will come out just fine.

**Nicholas:** Yes.

**Neil:** One thing we've learned is that the context of history, a generation can suddenly switch. Don't forget that the periods of George Bush Senior, and John Kennedy, and all those people, young men, World War II, in the late '30s, a lot of them were signing the Oxford Pledge, "Never enter a war again," and the day after Pearl Harbor they were all enlisting.

**Nicholas:** During the Second World War, there was a famous RAF Fighter Pilot, who got shot down many times and he actually lost both legs, had artificial legs put on, and got back in his Spitfire, and still flew. He was called Douglas Bader. He was a real hero of the time, and I heard a fascinating interview with him in the 1960s, when, of course, the new Boomer Generation were tearing up all the universities and disrespecting authority and so on, and someone said to him, "if the Second World War happened now, don't think this lot would be a shambles? They wouldn't be able to pull off what you did?"

I thought he was going to say, "yes" and he said, "Not at all." He said, "If you go back to the 1930s we were all behaving like that then. We didn't care about anything, having wild parties, drinking late, la-la-la." He said, "When the war came we all changed and we stepped up to the plate."

**Neil:** I must say, we have always believed when we had written about the G.I. Generation, that the GIs were different before the Great Depression, they were different before, they were already a very different Generation. They were put in uniforms when they were young, Boys Scouts, Girl Scouts, they were the first Miss Americas, and they were actually much better behaved on college campuses, than the Lost Generation was; that they were deeply, politically engaged in the Great Depression.

They were joining the unions, they were voting for FDR and all that. So they were very different well before World War II. We think rather that World War II galvanized that energy in a distinctive direction. Let me put it this way. We think the basic temperament of the Millennial Generation has shaped: teamwork, belief in collective specialness and all of that; confident, and optimistic about the future, and so forth; but the temperament has yet to be harnessed to a specific historical agenda.

I mean, that's what we are talking about, and as that happened then they say, "Okay, we are putting in our money, so to speak, we are putting our energy into this, we have to make this happen," but the temperament is shaped before. So I disagree in a sense, the sense that if you were at the Boomer Generation, and you had to go into something approximating World War II, actually it wouldn't have gone as well. We actually have had wars using awakening soldiers, an awakening military, and generally they have not been our greatest moments: things like the Spanish-American War, obviously the Vietnam War was a disaster; it was a disaster for morale, it was a disaster even on a tactical level. I mean, solders were frying each other, they were pulling a hand grenade and striking at each other, hence there was great animosity, there was rampant and drug use, there was no training of the troops, and one of the most incredible things that happened in the Vietnam War, is that we were rotating these young people because we didn't accept the idea of real sacrifice, right. This is where it's testing for all. No one was really going to suffer.

**Nicholas:** No.

**Neil:** What we were doing is, we were rotating kids in and out, and on very short term of duties, so your only goal was to get through this couple of months and not get hurt, and you'd be thrown back. In World War II, you went off, and you said, "No one is coming home until we win this thing." Do you know what I mean?

**Nicholas:** Yes.

**Neil:** No one is coming home. You are all going to be here until we go all the way to Berlin, or to Tokyo, very different mindset. That's says something, too, about who was leading, you know, the archetype of the leaders, right?

**Nicholas:** Yes. In your research you've talked about the new generations being no longer religious but being strongly spiritual, and I heard you say there was room for spiritual entrepreneurship, for something new to fill that space. I wonder; can you see the signs of what is going to fill that space?

**Neil:** Do you mean in terms of religion?

**Nicholas:** Yes, or spiritual stuff.

**Neil:** Or spirituality?

**Nicholas:** Beliefs and structures.

**Neil:** Right. Well, there's a very interesting rhythm in American history, and many of the historians of religion will point to this, and it's related to when I talked earlier about the great awakenings in American history, but these great awakenings have always been anti-institutional movements, and they've always been powered by the young. That's your prophet archetype, and typically the target of the young, are the veterans of the last great event. I mean that's just, again and again, a sequence that we see.

Coincident with this rhythm, is a rhythm between periods in which religion tends to bear in the direction of salvation by faith, and periods in which religion bears in the direction of salvation by works. The two great alternatives, and typically, during and after an awakening, we veer in the direction of salvation by faith. What matter is what's inside, and that's very much the Boomer approach.

Ruth Wade wrote a book called *Generation of Seekers, of Boomers and Religion*. Talked about Boomers who are constantly looking for whatever will satisfy this thing inside. He finally ends up calling the Boomers, I thought it was a great expression, he says, "They are a generation that believes in serial orthodoxy," which I thought was a wonderful expression. It termed it like serial monogamy, serial orthodoxy.

Whereas salvation by works on the other hand, says, "No, you know what really matters is how will religion actually helps people, helps the community," so basically, if you all go to church together, and we all work on things together to actually build this community, that's real charity, that's actually getting things done, as opposed to just being a hermit out in the monastery.

By the way, a hugely popular retirement pastime now for Boomers is to rent a room at some monastery, you know, to go meditate for a weekend or something. Doesn't that sound great? It makes yourself a better person. Your project is your soul; your project doesn't involve anyone else. These are very generationally related, as you can imagine. The millennial, the Hero archetype, typically brings back the idea of salvation by works.

They move away from the idea that religion should be somehow driven by guilt, what you feel inside, and more of the idea, and if you want to put this way, that religion should be driven a bit more by shame, what other people think of you. By the way, and if you think about the millennial they're using, social media and Facebook. Everyone is always looking at how you behave.

Do you ever think of the implications of that? Where we are moving back from guilt to shame, and I don't know how many Boomers I know who look at Facebook and they look what Millennials are doing online, and it reminds them of George Orwell in 1984. I mean, our biggest fear was Big Brother who is going to cameras in their homes, do you remember that? In 1984, these Millennials are putting their own cameras in their homes. Right, they're doing it themselves.

**Nicholas:** Yes. Last question is: what's going to happen to family life?

**Neil:** We think it's going to become much more functional, I think one of the emerging stories in American social life, which is already beginning to show through in the data, is how extremely well, generations get on today. It's an absolute surprise how well Millennials get along with their Boomer parents. They watch the same movies, they listen the same music, they save the same songs on their iPods; they wear the same brand name clothing. They're moving back into the same homes. We have a huge growth in America of multigenerational households.

One of the great surprises of the G.I. Generation, the greatest generation, and a real tragic sense of tragic surprise, is how distant they felt from their own kids during the consciousness revolution, because they had always been so close to their own parents and didn't understand when their own kids were so distant from them in values.

The surprise for Boomers is just the opposite. Why kids never leave us, they just stay right here, the come back and living in their 20s or age 30 they still live right next door, or they still live with us. They get along with us just great, we don't understand why. Why did it happen? I think actually it's typical of the Fourth Turning, that as history speeds up, challenges in the outer worlds speed up, our own personal life actually becomes less complicated.

**Nicholas:** Thank you so much for your time, Neil. I really appreciate it. If anyone wants to be in touch with you or study your research online what contact details would you recommend?

**Neil:** Just come to www.lifecourse.com, and we have up on that site, and you can easily find it, a blog which I'm going to continually ramping up over the next few months. We are going to have a lot of stuff going on there, running commentary on generations turning and generational-driven social trends.

**Nicholas:** Fantastic. Thank you very much.

**Neil:** Thank you, Nick.

# Catalyzing Change

## Engaging Emergence

**Peggy Holman interviewed by Dr Nicholas Beecroft**
Seattle based author and consultant, Peggy Holman, has helped explore a nascent field of social technologies that engage "whole systems" of people from organizations and communities in creating their own future. She is a recognized leader in deploying group processes that directly involve hundreds, or thousands, of people in organizations or communities in achieving breakthroughs.

In the second edition of The Change Handbook, Holman joins her co-authors to profile sixty-one innovative engagement processes used by organizations and communities to uncover creative responses to complex challenges. The book is the considered the definitive resource for leaders and consultants who work to increase resilience, agility, collaboration, and aliveness in their organizations and communities.

Peggy's latest book, Engaging Emergence: Turning Upheaval into Opportunity, won the 2011 Nautilus Gold Book Award for Conscious Business/Leadership. A roadmap for tackling complex challenges, Engaging Emergence provides stories, principles, and practices for inviting people to come together and turn disruptions into possibilities.

In this interview with Dr Nicholas Beecroft, Peggy gives her optimistic account of the emergence of a new Civilization by a broad base of people experimenting with new ways of being and doing. She describes how she thinks we can boost our cultural direction and self-confidence and sets out her highest vision for Western Civilization. She says what's great about America and the West right now-what we should preserve and build upon. She discusses the use of group processes to catalyze the evolution of our culture. Peggy believes that democracy is continuing to evolve for the better through increasing self-authorship. She describes Appreciative Inquiry, Open Space Technology and World Cafe. Peggy gives her view on how we can integrate the dark, shadow side of our history so as to unlock our power and potential.

**Nicholas:** Peggy Holman, welcome to the series Exploring the Future of Western Civilization.

**Peggy:** Thank you, Nicholas. It's great to be here with you.

**Nicholas:** Peggy lives in Seattle. She's an author and a consultant. Her specialism is in social technologies that engage whole systems, complex systems of people, whether it be communities, organizations, and she helps them go through a whole range of group processes to work out what is their future, their future vision, their future strategy, and she does this, anything from small groups all the way up to thousands of people engaging on complex problems.

She's worked in many places, but those include Boeing, Microsoft, the National Institute of Corrections, and the Bill and Melinda Gates Foundation. A few years back, she co-founded the organization Journalism that Matters, which is a national coalition of journalists, educators, and reformers who are trying to reshape news and the information ecosystem.

She became very prominent when she published her now famous book, The Change Handbook, which is like the bible of organizational change processes with 61 different processes outlined, kind of an off the shelf how to do it book, which is really useful.

Most recently, she wrote a book, Engaging Emergence, Turning Upheaval into Opportunity, which is a big picture book and she says that's a road map for tackling complex challenges, engaging emergence, and it provides stories, principles and practices for inviting people to come together and turn disruptions into possibilities. Welcome, Peggy.

**Peggy:** Thank you. As I said, it's great to be here. It's always interesting to hear my life through somebody else's speaking of it.

**Nicholas:** If that's not right, would you add or subtract to that?

**Peggy:** I think you covered it quite nicely.

**Nicholas:** Thank you.

**Peggy:** Thank you for that.

**Nicholas:** Can I start with a really big picture question, how can we, we being Western Civilization, how can we boost our Civilization sense of self-confidence and direction?

**Peggy:** That really is a big picture question. Actually, I'd like to answer it at two levels, in part because it's such a big question, it causes me to want to give a really simple, easily graspable step in and do it kind of answer. I want to answer at that level and then give a little larger picture answer.

My simplest answer is by asking good appreciative questions. I say that because ultimately, and you'll probably hear this theme throughout, if you look at patterns of change and how emergence occurs, which I would loosely define as order arising out of chaos, how it happens, it's always about the actions of local agents and that's you and me. What we do as individuals really does matter.

So much today of the influences of Western thinking is very much a problem-solution kind of orientation and because of that, we tend to become experts in our problems, and focus on them and go more deeply into them. The funniest thing, what research now tells us that we get more of what we focus on and our minds don't understand the knots. If we're focusing on having less violence or less of a bad effect on something, well, guess what, we get more of that and we've been doing that for quite a long time now.

At the level of the individual, if we start shifting the questions, and I do this a lot, of turning people's questions around, when somebody says, "How do we reduce the violence?" I'll say, "Well, how do we create a healthier community?" How do we turn the questions around so the more of us who are doing that, looking for the okay, what's possible now? That's my local answer.

**Nicholas:** Yes, actually, that question underpins this series because a few years ago, I was looking into the so-called War on Terror strategy about how are we going to win that, well, what are we going to do? Really, you can talk about what the others are doing and what we can do to stop them doing this.

The core question comes back to, well, who are we? How can we make our team so vibrant, dynamic, and successful that A, our own people want to be a part of it and it's really successful, and B, others want to join us and don't want to attack us? I noticed that that question wasn't really being asked very much.

**Peggy:** It's sad, but it isn't. It actually reminds me, several weeks after 9/11, I was actually part of a panel, and of course, people in the room were still shell-shocked from the experience. We found in part of this conversation, it was at a conference on change, people, someone asked, "How would you destroy a network like Al-Qaeda?" The thing that I realized and said in the moment is you don't. You make its purpose irrelevant. That kind of work I think fits with what you were just talking about. If we become an attractive, welcoming, open society that is curious about and able to embrace difference, we create the conditions where something like an Al-Qaeda becomes irrelevant.

Let me say a few words about my bigger picture answer to the question because I think in the practical context, asking great appreciative questions is hugely practical. Having a context for how change happens so that when we're faced with it, more of us are equipped to deal with it ourselves and bring others along with us can also make a difference.

I'd like to take a 50,000-feet level big picture look at how change occurs in actual systems, in social systems and it's a pattern that I think has been named in a variety of ways, and I have found it very useful to look at the entry point into change, which is always through disturbance. When you stop and think about it, it makes sense because, of course, if there were no disturbance, there'd be no need for change.

One of the lessons of that is when we're disrupted in some way, when something throws us off balance, our typical reaction and our understandable reaction is often resistance or denial or pushing back or trying to ignore it in some way. What happens is if we do those things, there's a high likelihood it won't go away. It will actually just get louder. The more we develop the capacity of relating to disruption by getting curious and learning about it, the more equipped we are to enter into change.

Then the pattern that follows from that entry point, and by the way, this happens whether we're conscious of it or not, but you often look at any kind of emergency situation, you have a huge disruption of some sort, a hurricane, an earthquake or even losing your job so it doesn't have to be man-made, and it can come from inside or outside the system that we're a part of, what happens is there is a sense of things falling apart, which of course puts us on an emotional roller coaster. What's going on is it's essentially the elements that made up the system that gave it its shape and coherence, its stability begin to unravel.

If we enter into this period of differentiation, of being able to experiment, to be able to look at the aspects that used to exist that we want to keep and those that weren't necessarily possible before and see what we want to embrace, we can discover the differences make a difference.

I do a lot of work with journalists. This is a field that is in the midst of tremendous upheaval and those who are in the midst of creating the new are having a wonderful time, an exciting time experimenting with how audience and interaction, and how to do investigation, and there are just a myriad of experiments. Ultimately, those threads start pulling together into some kind of coherent form. Now in journalism, that hasn't yet arisen, although we're beginning to see little bits of the shape. We know it's more of a conversation than a lecture for example.

Ultimately, from disruption, through differentiation, we end up with a new ideally higher order coherence that has more people or aspects of the system that weren't necessarily part of it before becoming part of it now. That to me, the more people who have a sense of that kind of shift, that wave pattern of change, the better equipped we are to have a sense of cultural direction and self-confidence.

**Nicholas:** Because it becomes easier to let go or open to the change because you understand it's a healthy natural process as opposed to catastrophe that needs to be stopped at all costs.

**Peggy:** Yes, and frankly, there may well be catastrophe in it. I mean this isn't about denying grief or fear or any of those things, they could well be a part of it. I can still have faith that there's something on the other side because by definition, there's mystery involved. If I knew what was on the other side, it's not emergent. It's not a change in the large sense of the term.

**Nicholas:** When you were talking about change and how we can relate to it in a way that embraces what's going on rather than being overwhelmed or resisting it. You're working with journalists, an important group who shape our group consciousness. Of course, another such group is politicians and whilst privately, some politicians might have the sort of belief system you're talking about, it's very difficult for them in our current, particularly in our current media climate to actually talk in that way because if they don't stand up and say, "I know absolutely everything. I know how everything works. I have all the answers. I'm super confident and this is exactly what we must do," or if they express the ambivalence or paradox or uncertainty that's absolutely core to what you're talking about, the media sets on them like a pack of dogs, don't they?

**Peggy:** It's an interesting challenge. I think both of those professions highly prize certainty and ultimately will change because the disruptions are getting louder. I hear through mainstream journalists, I hear the term unprecedented more and more, and I think we see the beginnings of changes in that arena happening and I listen for it. Certainly, the mainstream politicians do as you're saying. I listen for the voices of the few that are indeed willing to express a different perspective.

I actually in the years that I've been doing this work, I have run into exactly one elected official who gets and practices in his own work the kinds of civic engagement that we're talking about and he's a state senator from Hawaii. I think there's a whole arena around civic engagement that is gaining traction where if not the elected officials themselves, other government agencies that deal with the public are looking for more productive, more effective ways of engaging people, the citizenry in finding answers.

**Nicholas:** Could you give an example of that, of where that's been successful?

**Peggy:** Actually, what's coming to mind is the work of Robert Putnam. He wrote a pretty well-known book called ...

**Nicholas:** Bowling Alone.

**Peggy:** Bowling Alone, which correlated social activity with declining civic involvement. A number of years later, I think eight or nine years later, he came out with a book, Better Together, where he profiled I think 8 or 10 different locations. I think they were all in the U.S., but what he found were areas where the public had an active role and actually, had funds to be able to make decisions, kept them engaged not only locally, but on all levels of politics.

For example, in the City of Portland, Oregon, apparently, Oregon state law puts aside some tax revenues for local communities to do their work and they redesigned their roadways, putting more circles through this kind of civic engagement activity. There's a small example.

**Nicholas:** We started with one big picture question. Now can I go with the next? What is your highest vision for Western Civilization or possibly global Civilization?

**Peggy:** You do ask big questions, I must say, Nicholas.

**Nicholas:** Well, you're a big picture person.

**Peggy:** Yes, I have been accused of that, yes. I think that we have such potential and I think that as I looked at that question, I think a society in which the needs of individuals and the needs of the whole are met is kind of my simple encapsulation of my vision. I say that because when I first got into the work of working with whole systems, one of the turning point moments for me was I when was with a group in a company and I saw something.

It was highly contentious situation because labor and management contract negotiations were going on in the background and I saw something that I didn't know was possible in that moment, which was that the needs of the people in the room, the individuals in the room, and the needs of the organization and the needs of the unions could all be met. Until I had experienced that, I always thought that one or the other had to sacrifice, that it was always a tradeoff.

What I've discovered is that when we create the conditions where people bring the best of who they are where there's room for their fullest expression of what matters most to them, that this is interesting and it's almost contradictory because it seems like that would create the conditions for wild chaos and in fact, because as humans we draw from the same deeper core in human values, ultimately, through having the space to express our deepest desires, we begin to discover there are places of connection and a kind of wholeness emerges that makes room for what matters most and serves. In the process, we begin to feel a sense of connection to each other. In that moment, there's a shift that takes place when people begin to feel their connection not just to each other, but to a larger sense of wholeness. We actually become a social body.

At that point, to undermine that social body is like cutting off your own hand and so our behavior shifts. In that sense, while it doesn't sound like much on the surface to say well, the needs of the individual, the needs of the whole are both met, my experience has been in working with a microcosm of an organization or a community, when those conditions exist, we treat each other differently, we listen differently, we cut each other way more slack, and our basic assumptions about each other's actions, even if they go awry are to check out what the intentions, the underlying intentions really were.

**Nicholas:** I can see how that works in a small group. You're creating a safe space and getting people to know each other and you could bring together the most extreme opposites and see how they would be able to get on, but when they then leave the conference or the therapy room or the consulting room or whatever, and then go back to the wider system, what conditions are necessary in a big picture, in a whole organization or a city or a country for that shift you just talked about to take hold and not slip back to the old more divisive way?

**Peggy:** This may sound overly simple-practice. There is something about having that experience once that's magical. Having the chance to do it again starts to cause people to think huh, maybe that wasn't just a fluke. The more we do it, the more able we are to do it ourselves, to have confidence it isn't just an accident and to begin to ask the questions of how do I get more of this. It's about creating a virtuous cycle.

One of the things that gives me hope and frankly, conditions could go either way. I am an optimist. I do think that we are on the beginning of an awakening of a different kind of consciousness, which has this greater awareness of ourselves, seeing ourselves in context. I think part of that brings with it that shift from a problem-solution kind of orientation to a possibility orientation.

Goodness knows, we're all going to slip back. Certainly, I have my moments of doubt as well though they're fewer than they used to be. There really is something about not just doing this once, but picking yourself up, dusting yourself off whenever you find yourself in a place of doubt or despair and finding some place in it where you can ask a question that says, "Okay, yes, all that's going on. Now what and what can I do?"

**Nicholas:** I've heard you talk about, well, you've been talking about the emergence of something new, and as we were discussing before we got started, it's very easy to come up with a massive long list of all the disasters and terrible things and threats and all the rest of it, but what are the positive fresh shoots coming through? What are the first signs of some emerging new positive Civilization that you see through your experience?

**Peggy:** It's a great question. Actually, I'm thinking about a story from a journalist I did some work with. Actually, several journalists have said variations on this. One, a career journalist said at the opening of an event I was doing with journalists, "I got tired of being depressed all the time so I decided to go look for something that was working," and she said, "Once I started looking, I could find things everywhere." Interestingly enough, I heard almost that identical statement from another journalist who said, "We need a beat, a reporter's beat on change whether you're looking at philanthropy or healthcare or education, I would challenge to look out your own window and your own surroundings."

For example, in the world of finance, the Grameen Bank micro-lending experiment that's pulling people out of poverty in developing countries and is now making its way into places like the U.S. in areas that are highly poverty stricken. You can look at the Slow Food Movement that is growing in terms of more locally grown food and weaving a tighter net of community.

I just was in an area on a place called Whidbey Island that's near where I live where over the last 10 years, this is a community that has built an extraordinary social safety net through the initiative of individuals in the community where they've created things like a food bank that looks more like a grocery store and put the resources in place to start training the next generation of farmers because the average age of farmers in this country is in their early 60s, which is kind of a daunting thought as we think about where our food comes from.

You can look at the educational system and there are some really stellar experiments. There was a wonderful experiment using appreciative inquiry with kids that had been classified as high risk for dropping out of high school. What they did was they started asking these kids what does it mean to you to be a leader? What they found was kids weren't necessarily interested in learning. They were very interested in being good leaders and it changed their attitude towards learning and gave them a different context to understand what learning was about and why it was important, and they ended up with something like a 97% graduation rate.

**Nicholas:** Part of the purpose of appreciative inquiry is to say what's already great about the way things are. Regarding Western Civilization or maybe America if you want to narrow it down, what already is fantastic and what's worth preserving and cherishing?

**Peggy:** Again, you ask such bold questions. I found myself as I contemplate that question what immediately pops to mind is the creative spirit that's in us all. I think Western Civilization is particularly noted for better and worse, in a sense the Newtonian revolution, and the themes that we have been able to create out of stuff. The fact that you and I can be talking over and seeing each other over the extraordinary distance is a tribute to the kind of creativity that has created longer lives.

I think they have to date been healthier lives although we are beginning to feel the consequences of the downside of the way we've gone about that creativity such as rising rates in cancer and so forth. As I think about what's best in who, what we are, I say arts and culture, and our creative ability to do, to make both stuff, and deepen the connections across many cultures, and that one of our challenges in the coming era is to learn how to do that, be more mindfully connected with the systems of which we are a part, knowing that we don't do any of that in a vacuum.

**Nicholas:** Thank you for that. As an American, I expected you to say freedom and democracy in that list. Maybe you just missed it off by mistake or maybe there's a reason for that. Given your deep knowledge of change processes and engaging people, how can we deepen and enrich our democracy so it isn't just a small cabal of people manipulating the media to get a vote and then they go away and do what they like for four years? Democracy didn't start 200 years ago and then it's done. It's something we can do better. How can we improve it?

**Peggy:** It's a really, really important question and it's funny, I think that Greece is the birthplace of democracy. It didn't pop to mind for me, but I think that democracy is part of an evolutionary process in terms of how humans organize themselves to get stuff done.

There's an interesting book. Are you familiar with Howard Zinn's work? He's a sociologist. A People's History of the U.S. and I believe there's also one that's A People's History of the World.

It's sort of a socialist view of history. He would probably object to that characterization, but it's basically in reading his sweep of history, he'll talk about how the people who are typically in power get their way. Then the people rise up and things improve and more people have more freedom. Then people in power slash them again and you can watch this trend over 400 years of history.

His writing is actually kind of depressing to read and yet at the end of the book when I sat back and looked at it, what I realized is that there's a trend in how we govern ourselves towards increasing self-authorization in the way it gets done. That to me is the direction that we're going. I think the tools that enable us to connect many to many across distances are going to make a huge difference in supporting our ability to do that.

I go back to the thing that I said at the very beginning about needs of the individuals and needs of the whole because I believe that part of the evolution of being able to stand in our certainty as a doorway into engaging with uncertainty, calls for each of us as individuals to bring forth our voices more fully. I've talked about that a little bit. In a culture where that becomes normative, we become, I like to use the term, a differentiated whole that it has in its nature the tension of that both and of whole voice individual expression while feeling connected to the other. I think the patterns of democracy, the capacities to be in dialogue are where those shifts are going.

Frankly the legal system that we in the States inherited from you is an advocacy-based system. It's based in win-lose and ultimately, we need to make the shift towards a dialogically-based system, one where the emphasis is on inquiry and thinking together across our differences.

I've always found it intriguing that the shape of the U.S. Congress is a semi-circle and I know that Benjamin Franklin was ambassador to the Iroquois nation, one of the First Nations people who understood circular forms of dialogue, that instead of many native cultures sitting around the fire in the circle that they would talk and talk and talk until there was nothing more to say and then, they would go act. The talk didn't even necessarily directly relate to the actions to be taken and yet at the end of that exploration, people knew there were rules, they knew how they fit into the larger system, and they were able to act from that perspective.

Anyway, that's a full circle and I always had the feeling that, and Benjamin Franklin brought many of the aspects of the democratic system that we use today, the checks and balances and so forth from the Iroquois nation, what he learned from them. I always figured with the sort of semicircular seating, he got it half-right. Somehow marrying it with an advocacy system based in win-lose, he cut off that ability to talk with people who see the world differently.

What I have observed over and over in working with groups around dialogue, I find in that is when your impulse is to say to somebody, "I disagree with that and here's why," it's a great moment to stop that impulse, take a breath and instead say something like, "That's an interesting perspective. Tell me more about that." Then really listen and listen to understand not to be able to make a better case to debate the person and beat them at their own game because guaranteed they won't tell you twice if you use what they tell you in that way.

There are wonderful stories of bringing people of different political persuasions together. The Truth and Reconciliation Commission I think is a wonderful example of bringing together people with very different world views who in that case where you were dealing with situations of death and violence and deep antipathy there in Northern Ireland where people actually could sit across each other and speak truth to each other, feel heard and be heard. That aspect in our democratic process, bringing the dialogic in I think is the most critical shift that we could make in how we relate to people with different perspectives.

Actually, what I know is that breakthrough answers happen because there are seeds of truth in every point of view. It's like the whole conservative-progressive kind of tension that I think exists in most countries. I hear the arguments in my own country about bigger government. Nobody wants bigger government. We want a government that's the size to do what we need it to do and no more. Of course, organizations have a way of continuing to grow so we need checks and balances on them. What it is that we want to conserve that is useful about the role that we want government to play? Having the conversation about what's the role of government and, therefore, how do we fund it is a far more useful dialogue than arguing over bigger or smaller.

One last thing I'll mention, there may be an equivalent in your country.

There's an organization in the States and in Canada, the National Coalition for Dialogue and Deliberation that is a terrific resource because its focus is using the kinds of conversational practices that have been at the core of my own work and learning about these kinds of shifts in social systems, but that it has its emphasis on civic engagement. They are just a terrific resource for working with government and communities in dealing with questions important for civil society.

**Nicholas:** Peggy, you're an expert in group process and in change. How can we create a group process which will spread like a virus, a positive virus, self-propagating throughout Western Civilization to rejuvenate it, to engage the people, to get them excited about who are we, where are we going, and what's our vision for the future and how do we make things better? What could that look like?

**Peggy:** In many ways, like many of the questions you're asking, it's a daunting question that I'm going to give you in many ways a pretty much simple answer to because I believe that that is already underway. It's underway in a way that isn't about a single process. This is a very, very complex multi-faceted challenge and as such, there are people who are approaching it each from their own point of view, each from their own place of passion, and attracting others to them. They're experimenting and failing and dusting themselves off, picking themselves up, trying it again, but people of good heart, which is virtually all of us who are asking what can I do to make a better place.

There's a principle I'd say at the heart of what it takes for us as individuals and as a collective to deal with the emergent nature of change and evolution, and it's to me what's at the heart of one of the practices that's been most influential in my own work, Open Space Technology. The way that I come to frame it through the influence of friends and colleagues is to take responsibility for what we love as an act of service.

Now there's a whole lot packed into that phrase. For one, it goes to something that we've been talking about all along. The notion of paying attention to what you love and sometimes it's phrased as where does my passion meet the needs of the world? Truly to ask yourself that question and encourage others to ask themselves that question, and in answering it, to act from that place, and my discovery is that when we do that, it truly becomes an act of service because we all are drawing from a core set of human needs to belong, to be able to contribute, to feel safety in which to raise a family. There are just some basic things that matter to all of us.

The more of us who liberate ourselves to act from that place, the more we will find our partners and the more we begin a virtuous cycle in the midst of the kind of collapse of the assumptions of the way things have been. As those break down, there are a thousand blossoms blooming. Everything from the Transition Town Movement or the Occupy Movement or the Arab Spring or look anywhere, there's revolutions in healthcare, there are revolutions in education. No matter what area you look at, there are people experimenting with new ways of operating. For me, those are the group processes.

**Nicholas:** Yes. I noticed that you took an interest in the Occupy Movement by getting involved in a think called Occupy Cafe. Have you got involved in the Tea Party Movement? That's a slightly naughty question, isn't it?

**Peggy:** Honestly, I haven't, and my involvement with Occupy was because of an invitation. Had I gotten an invitation from a Tea Party person, I would've shown up.

**Nicholas:** Is there a way that the Tea Party and the Occupy Movement could come together in a transpartisan way that would be synergistic, in service of the whole?

**Peggy:** That's such a fabulous question and I saw a diagram that made me laugh again because of its simplicity. It was a Venn diagram, two intersecting circles. For the Tea Party, the circle is labeled distrust in big government and for the Occupy Movement it's labeled distrust in big business. Guess what? There's this huge overlap of distrust at the intersection of big government and big business. I think there's a tremendous realm for people to come together.

**Nicholas:** What's their overlapping bubble on what they do trust? I bet they're quite similar, too, probably.

**Peggy:** It could well be. That's an interesting question, not one I've heard asked and not one I've asked myself. There's a funny thing about that. I have a friend who home schools his children and he was telling me that it's a place where kind of those extremes kind of circle around and meet because the people who homeschool children tend to be very progressive or fundamentalist in their religious point of view.

Well, guess what? They have common cause around the wellbeing of their children. Here you have these groups that may be politically at odds suddenly finding themselves as parents together. In that discovery of our common humanity, new things can blossom. I think we'll see more of those kinds of strange bedfellows coming together because there's a place at which the extremes start looking more like each other than they know.

**Nicholas:** Yes. You mentioned right at the beginning September the 11th, Al-Qaeda, you've also mentioned the Arab Spring. We're familiar with seeing the Islamic world or the Arab world as a threat. Is it possible to see them as a positive stimulus, a positive challenge or a synergistic learning experience, something that will get us to step up and renew ourselves, be stronger, be better, learn from their strengths or at the very least, stretch ourselves to be better?

**Peggy:** I certainly hope so. I actually suspect that some of the impetus and inspiration behind the Occupy Movement itself is because of the Arab Spring. I think it already has been an inspiration. It actually got me thinking about the time that was going on, I spent some time in South Africa and spent a day in Soweto learning some of the story of the end of apartheid in South Africa. Shortly before that, I'd actually been in a place called Greensboro, North Carolina, which is sometimes called the birth of the Civil Rights Movement in the US.

Something that struck me in all three of these examples, whether it's the Arab Spring, Soweto and the end of apartheid in South Africa or the civil rights movement in this country, all of them, the role of young people in being the spark for change. I've been thinking about that a lot as well. We have an interesting time where we've got the protesters of the '60s bringing their knowledge and skill of street organizing together with the tech savvy 20- and 30-somethings of today, when put together, the potential to create something new and something better increases.

I'm reminded of Fred Pollock, I think he was from the Netherlands. He's a social science researcher in the '50s and he studied the rise and fall of Civilizations. One of the things that he found was you can predict the end of a Civilization within a generation when it no longer has a positive image of its own future. It's really profound when you think about it.

**Nicholas:** Yes, well, that's driving my interest in doing this, exactly that, yes.

**Peggy:** Yes.

**Nicholas:** That's really fascinating. It's amazing hearing you both talk about generations and about South Africa. It's completely unsolicited yet those two themes run through all of these interviews, not because I've initiated them. There's something about the South African story, which has really touched people and really is obviously part of Western Civilizational mentality. Fascinating. Also, yes, the generation thing is fundamental.

Can I ask Peggy, how do we integrate our dark side? I'm a psychiatrist. I've got some ideas about doing that on an individual basis, but at a group level, how do we integrate those dark parts of our history or dark parts of our culture, the obvious things being past abuses or racism or differences in power. Those would be classic, but there are probably lots of others.

I was talking to some Germans earlier today about how they've got a long way to go in reconnecting their parts. They've gone through their process of apology for the past, remorse, guilt and shame and so on, but they've kind of left themselves in a rather broken state of okay, but what's next? Where's your healthy positive vision of who you are? You need to put yourself back together again and be healthy. From your group process experience, how do we do that at a group level?

**Peggy:** I think we need to talk to each other. It's a really, really important question and it's a funny one because as you've heard recurring theme in what I'm saying coming from a possibility orientation, there is something about being present and unattached. I don't mean unattached as I don't care, but unattached in the Buddhist way of being present too without allowing it to hook you. The gift that we owe each other is to be witnesses for each other.

A number of years ago, I think it was 2004, I co-hosted a conference called the Practice of Peace, and actually even its history, what inspired it, Harrison Owen who created Open Space Technology was invited to Rome with 25 Israelis and 25 Palestinians. All these 50 people were flown to Rome because it wasn't safe to do this in Israel. They spent 3 days in Open Space with each other around the issue of trust.

At the end of it, frankly, one of the things Harrison came away with was the insight that when we're faced with conflict, where our impulse is to shut down and close in, in fact, what we need to do is open more space to ask the question that allows us to step in. In a sense, that kind of work is an example to me of the work that needs to be done.

What we found, anyway, that event coupled with some others led to hosting this conference here. We had people from conflict zones around the world from Bosnia and Northern Ireland and Haiti and Nepal and Nigeria, inner cities, neighborhoods in the U.S. We had First Nations people. It was a very interesting mix.

We had Israeli and Palestinian, and this Palestinian woman showed a video of the building of the wall around the West Bank because that was fresh at that time, and it led to this very respectful heated exchange between the Israelis and the Palestinians because they felt that the video while attempting to show both sides, really didn't capture the fear that many Israelis felt that led to the building of the wall. The room witnessed that conversation. As it wound down, nobody tried to fix it. Nobody tried to intervene. The people in the room, there were 60 or 70 of us simply witnessed, held the container for that exchange to take place.

As it wound down without answers, a man from Northern Ireland stood up and talked about witnessing his sister being shot in a drive-by shooting. The man from Burundi who was there spoke of witnessing his village being wiped out. Several others spoke, the conditions that they had witnessed and been part of in their own countries, and the people of course who had come here were people who were seeking what's on the other side of that dark place that you're talking about. Again, no one tried to fix it or make it go away or do anything except listen.

The interesting thing was the next morning, there was a spirit of joy and celebration that was extraordinary. People came away with what they said that event has ripples to this day, people came away from that experience more affirmed in themselves, in their own capacity to go back in and be witness for those who were still angry or still hurting, and be able to provide for them a kind of deep listening that we as a group were able to provide for them. We all have work to do.

**Nicholas:** Yes, yes. I certainly experienced that a lot as a junior doctor, doing the unpleasant job of being on the emergency team in psychiatric hospitals, when the bleep goes, running towards violence, which is the last thing I would normally choose to do. Obviously, first of all, you have to have security. It has to be made safe, physically safe for everyone to be present, but once that is done, simply connecting and making rapport with the person who is apparently the aggressor and really genuinely listening.

I'd say 9 out of 10 times, that would resolve the issue and move you on and I'd be having a cup of tea with them not long after. Underneath was usually fear, shame, feeling not heard, feeling disrespected, those kind of things, sometimes imagined and sometimes true, but it really struck me how dealing with violence, that that work is a solution very effectively most of the time, but you must have security. You can't do that if it's not safe.

**Peggy:** Safe space definitely makes a difference. This popped through my head several times on the subject that we're talking about now. A colleague of mine, Mark Jones described a process, a very simple diagnostic in the context that we're talking about that he calls the HiSL, which stands for hear, see and love. The idea is that we need to HiSL everyone including ourselves.

The story behind it is he had an audience with the Dalai Lama in which he asked, "How do we teach the children peace?" The Dalai Lama said to him, "We all need to be heard, seen and loved or mischief occurs."

Mark went home and he started observing and studying behavior and experimenting with it. What he found was that when people don't feel heard, they shout or they shut up. If they don't feel seen, then they get in your face and they turn into a bully or they become invisible. If they don't feel loved, they do this kind of approach-avoid of coming in and then stepping back and coming and stepping back.

What he found is in each case, the remedy is in the quality of listening. He invites people, now that you've heard of the HiSL, it's time to experiment it, join the experiment. Something that I have found is when I run into somebody who's really cranky or biting in some way, rather than reacting to it, what goes through me now is oh, they're not feeling heard or they're not feeling seen. I'll respond to that perhaps with a question or a naming of, "Oh, gosh, I can tell that something just rattled you recently. You want to talk about it or whatever?" I'll listen to the deeper place and interact with that.

**Nicholas:** As you're talking there, one of the threads that runs through Western Civilization both domestically and overseas, well, particularly domestically are the hot topics of race, of immigration, of racism, and more recently, the Islamic aspect as well. I see political correctness as being like shadow prejudice. It's shadow racism. It's just turned on its head. Anti-fascism is fascism. It's the same thing, just as violent and so on. Of course, well meaning, but in terms of is it effect, does it achieve the desired aim? I would say does the opposite. Political correctness and multicultural ideology and the laws that we have in Europe, I don't know if you have them in America, which actually make it illegal to have robust democratic conversations about issues of race and religion which, democratically, is insane. In terms of evolution and emergence and what you were just saying, being heard is nuts, isn't it.

What needs to be done at the Civilizational level for us to let go of those kind of fascist, antifascist solutions, which are shadow racism and shadow imperialism, and actually own our racism, own our imperialism and really when I say that, I'm talking to people who call themselves liberals, but actually carry a lot of shadow racism and shadow imperialism and project it onto other people?

How can we drop those false structures and laws and actually enable people to engage in the positive healing process of HiSL, being heard, being seen, being listened to actually genuinely healing the wounds, genuinely overcoming the problems, and actually moving to a healthy conscious positive state beyond all of that kind of old pathology?

**Peggy:** Big questions. The legal barriers are a challenge that we don't face in this country. The First Amendment of our Constitution is the notion of free speech fortunately helps in that realm as much as it does in a variety of others. The legal question is not one that I have a lot of insight into.

I guess the main thing I can say, like any form of civil disobedience, it takes somebody willing to begin and to reach out across the lines of cultural or race or difference, and engage in the conversations as we were just saying.

I'm thinking about yet another South African story. The scenario planning work that happened, I think it was before Mandela was released, a group of South Africans from across all strata of that society came together to develop four possible scenarios for the future of the country. There was no judgment put on right or wrong or better or worse. The notion was what are the assumptions that we think are likely and picking a couple of those, then playing out the scenarios.

They landed in four scenarios and they had different names of birds for them. One was a scenario in which they end up isolated by the rest of the world and in essence implode because of the kinds of financial embargoes that were placed on them. Another, they become a populist country and, basically, anyone with any resources flees. There was only one of the four scenarios, which was basically about finding a way to work together that actually led to a future that was desirable.

There was never any voting or debating. It was simply a matter of this very different group of people talking. I guess where I'm going is what made me think of the story is when there's something more important to us than the differences or the prejudices that we hold, that it takes us together to create, then people join forces. It's back to my example of the strange bedfellows of people homeschooling their kids with radically different beliefs, but a higher purpose of their children. I think that's ultimately what will bring us together.

**Nicholas:** Is there anything that we haven't covered that you would like to say regarding the big picture question of how do we revitalize Western Civilization?

**Peggy:** I'll just reiterate something. I think I've said this, I just think it's so important. It happens a person at a time and the more each of us acts from the place of our own deep longing and caring, the more we will find we're not alone and find our partners, and create the virtuous cycle that I believe we are already in.

**Nicholas:** Fantastic, Peggy. Thank you. Very finally, if someone would like to follow your work, look at your books and maybe get in touch, how would you recommend them do that?

**Peggy:** You can visit my website, peggyholman.com and you can reach me at peggy@peggholman.com

**Nicholas:** Thank you very much, Peggy.

**Peggy:** You're welcome, Nicholas. Good to meet you. Thanks so much.

# Successful Nations

## Harnessing the Aspirations of the People

**Richard Barrett interviewed by Dr Nicholas Beecroft**
Richard Barrett is an author, speaker and social commentator on the evolution of human values in business and society. Richard's latest book is Love, Fear and the Destiny of Nations; the impact of the evolution of human consciousness on world affairs. Richard is a leading global expert on the evolution of human values, culture, leadership and consciousness in business and society.

Richard gives his assessment of Western Civilization-where we are, what's working well, the challenges we face and his vision for the next evolutionary steps into ever deeper democracy. His model of values driven leadership, leadership development and conscious evolution has been honed over thousands of leaders and organizations globally. He shows how this can be applied at the national and civilizational level.

He believes that there is an inevitable evolution of human values and consciousness once people's deficiency needs are met and they become able to expand their consciousness and values into seeking their growth needs. He is certain that China will evolve its own form of democracy within 20 years, as will those other nations which are learning from the West how to lift people out of poverty and the basic levels of deficiency needs.

In the West, he sees our next stage of development is to continue to create conditions in which people's basic needs are met so that we can evolve from freedom through equality, accountability, openness, transparency to trust. He says that business leaders are already well engaged in developing themselves to make this leap because they watch successful people and learn. He calls on political leaders to do the same but laments the current political culture which he feels is holding back our development.

Visit valuescentre.com and RichardBarrett.net

**Nicholas:** Richard Barrett, welcome to the series exploring the Future of Western Civilization.

**Richard:** Thank you. Happy to be here with you.

**Nicholas:** By way of introduction to Richard, for anyone who hasn't met him before, Richard is an author, a speaker, and a social commentator on the evolution of human values in business and society. He is very well known for being the founder and chairman of the Barrett Values Center, and is an internationally recognized thought leader on values, culture, leadership and consciousness. He is a fellow of the Royal Society of Arts, a visiting lecturer at the Consulting and Coaching for Change Leadership Course run by the University of Oxford and also in Paris, and he is an adjunct professor at the Royal Roads University, the Institute for Values Based Leadership. He is visiting lecturer at the One Planet MBA at Exeter University, and is the creator of the internationally recognized Cultural Transformational Tools, which are being used in 60 countries around the world, supporting more than 3,000 major organizations and leaders on their transformational journeys. He's a fellow of the World Business Academy and a former values coordinator of the World Bank. Most recently, I'm very privileged that Richard has given me an advanced copy of his new book, called *Love, Fear, and the Destiny of Nations: The Impact of the Evolution of Human Consciousness on World Affairs*. Thank you very much for agreeing to join this series, Richard.

**Richard:** I'm very happy to participate.

**Nicholas:** Let me just kick off with the state of play. What is the state of Western Civilization?

**Richard:** When I started writing *Love, Fear, and the Destiny of Nations* in its final form about nine months ago, I was really quite optimistic about the evolution of Western society. As I got deeper and deeper into the book, I became more pessimistic. However, the optimism has resurfaced.

The state of Western Civilization. It's a good question, because I have to look at that question from the perspective of evolution. Evolution has been going on, as we know, for four billion years, and at the cosmic level for fourteen billion years, and what's happening right now with human consciousness is, for me, the cutting edge of evolution. *Homo sapiens* carry the arrow of evolution forward, and it's the consciousness of *Homo sapiens* that is really at the forefront of evolution right now.

Whatever we see going on the world, at a national, regional, and global level, in terms of the way that society is being organized, is really evolution happening before our very eyes. When you say, "What is the state of Western Civilization," I have to look at it from that perspective. I look at it from evolution as the evolution of human consciousness.

So where are we? I have a model, the Seven Levels of Consciousness model, that is based on Maslow's theory, with a difference. It looks at consciousness rather than needs. We're about halfway up the seventh level. We've got to the point where nations are what I would call "individuating," becoming independent; where people in nations are beginning to embrace transformation. What we see, for example, in the Arab Spring movement, is people in a nation getting to the point where they've met their deficiency needs after survival, relationship, and self-esteem needs, and now are seeking to satisfy their growth needs.

Democracy is a major stepping point, I think, in the evolution of human consciousness at the group level. You could say that, for an individual, individuation is really important. That means letting go of the beliefs that you learned during your childhood in the cultural conditions, beliefs that no longer serve you, sometimes the fear-based beliefs, and embracing your own beliefs and becoming true to who you are. That's individuation. Well that individuation is happening with the masses with nations all over the world. It's because they've got to the point where they've been able to meet their deficiency needs: survival, relationship, and self-esteem. As we've had this improvement in living conditions, as we've had this improvement in incomes, people have begun to be able to meet those deficiency needs and say, "Well what's next? My growth needs." They are stepping into their growth needs in these authoritarian nations and saying, "We want democracy." Basically, what they're asking for is freedom from fear.

That's what individuation is at a personal level, and that's, I think, what is happening in the world globally. People are transforming and saying, "I want freedom from fear: Freedom from my own personal fear," that's personal evolution, "Freedom from fear of the regime in which I live," and that's societal evolution. Actually, there are not that many full democracies. Democracies are on a sort of continuum and if you look at the Economic Intelligence Unit, they have their Democracy Index. You can find it on Wikipedia. What you see there is, there's only 26 nations that are full democracies. Democracy is a fragile concept, I believe. It's evolving, but it's evolving slowly. Well, "Slowly" ... It's all happened in the last hundred years, so that's relatively fast, in one way.

We're at that point where people all over the world are beginning to say, "Enough is enough. I want to have the freedom to design my life, individually, and we want the freedom to design our lives, collectively." So we're seeing this upsurge in democracy happening all over the world. It's an amazing moment in evolution, actually. It's absolutely awe-inspiring for me, to see evolution in action. When I read the newspaper, some of the topics are evolution in action. I find that tremendously exciting.

**Nicholas:** Brilliant. To start off with an appreciative question, in Western Civilization right now, what already is working really well? What's the success upon which we build?

**Richard:** Wow. What's the success? The success that we have comes from two factors. The first factor is the fact that we've been able to create, over the past 200 years, since the Industrial Revolution, we've been able to allow or create the conditions in which the masses can meet their deficiency needs. Up to that point, it was all the elites; and the elites governed and controlled everything. Just a mere factor of how allowing people, or making the conditions so that people could meet their deficiency needs by improving their levels of income, brings them through to the point where they now want to meet their growth needs. That is when they start to ask for democracy.

First of all, the improvement in living conditions, the alleviation of poverty is the first factor, and the second factor is that has led to this outburst of democracy, and I think that is the second most important factor to say what's been successful in Western Civilization.

It's not just Western Civilization, in my opinion, because I don't make the distinction between east and west. Every human being is a human being, having this physical experience on the planet. Basically, our human needs are all the same, whether we live in the West or the East. However, our approach to life, and the value and beliefs we hold, could be different for Western Civilization than Eastern Civilization. I see these coming together; slowly, but coming together.

**Nicholas:** This process of cultural evolution: Do you think that it is a deterministic thing? Is it something like a seed it's growing and naturally unfolding, and there is a natural path? Or do you think that it's something that's either intentionally generated through creativity and through strategy, through consciousness, and is it something that could unfold? Is it something necessarily that we carry on advancing forward? Could it all fall in on itself or go backwards or sideways?

**Richard:** There is a sense in which things can move forwards and backwards, but there is an overall pattern. For me, there is an overall pattern to evolution, that, actually, has been going on for fourteen billion years. I spent two or three years trying to figure out, what is the pattern to evolution. A big part of the book, *Love, Fear, and the Destiny of Nations*, at least the beginning part, is identifying the patterns of evolution. I wrote about that in my last book, *The New Leadership Paradigm*, as well.

What I identified was, first of all, when we're talking about evolution, we have to recognize that it's not just physical evolution, because as species have evolved, then minds have evolved. For me, evolution is just as much about consciousness as it is about physical forms. The consciousness determines how we deal with survival situations, how we deal with the things that are happening around us. As evolution progressed into different forms, the manner in which we handled survival situations or complex situations or threatening situations evolved, too. *Homo sapiens* represents the pinnacle of that.

Now let me get to these three universal stages of evolution. This applies to atoms, to cells, to all creatures, and to *Homo sapiens*. The first principle is you have to become viable and independent in your framework of existence. If you're not viable and independent, you're gone.

Second principle, as your framework conditions become more threatening to your survival, what happens is, you bond with other viable independent entities to create the group structure, and that gives you more resilience, individually and collectively.

The third stage of universal evolution is, when conditions become even more complex and more threatening, what happens is those group structures cooperate with each other to form a higher-order entity. That is how evolutions progress. So we have atoms became vital and independent. They bonded to form group structures, molecules. Molecules cooperated to create a higher-order entity called a "cell." Cells became viable and independent, bonded to create group structures, organisms. Organisms cooperated, created a creature. One of those creatures, *Homo sapiens*, you and I are examples of that, I hope, tried to become viable independent, in other words, to individuate and self-actualize. We're bonding together to form group structures. Those group structures are nations, and as conditions are becoming more complex, we're recognizing that those nations have to cooperate in order to create the next higher-level entity, or to survive, because the problems of existence are now global, but the systems and the processes we have for dealing with that are national.

Is there a pattern to evolution? Absolutely. There are three universal stages of evolution. If you take those three universal stages and apply it to *Homo sapiens*, you have a pattern for the future of human destiny and societal destiny. That's basically that pattern, and this is what this book is about, says the pattern follows the three universal stages. As we are now beginning to bond together to form nations, first of all we bonded together to form bands, tribes, city-states, and now nations, those nations are learning to cooperate to create a higher-order entity.

That higher-order entity comes in two stages. The first stage is to create a higher-order entity at a regional level, like the European Union, and then, what I foresee is that we'll have other regional entities. They exist all over the world, there's the Arab League, for example, and there are other regional entities. These entities will get stronger and stronger. Then they will cooperate with each other to create the higher-order entity, which we will call a global governance system. Because we can't solve the problems we've got with the structures we've got right now. So I foresee global governance, but I see it in two stages: first regional governance and then global governance.

**Nicholas:** With what you've just described, in terms of global evolution, it's obviously true from an observational perspective. We can look across our own British or Western history and we can look in other countries, and it does appear that that pattern is what we're observing. Put it this way: I met some Chinese diplomats some years ago, when they were trying to persuade the Americans not to weaponize space. They said to me, "Look, this democracy thing that you keep talking about, that's a Western idea. It's got no relevance to us. We have our own type of democracy." They described how their own Communist Party has all sorts of consensus and dialogue and so on. They said, "You mustn't try to force your path upon us. We're going to do things in our own way."

In the last few years, given that our economy is struggling and we've got some real challenges, and the Chinese are doing incredibly well in a whole range of ways, they're getting more and more assertive in saying, "We're not going to follow your path. There's the Chinese way." We have heard that before, with the Japanese or others. Is that just rhetoric or wishful thinking? Or might they be right?

**Richard:** Democracy is a fluid concept. You can go all the way from an electoral democracy to a full liberal democracy. When nations begin to move from authoritarian regime, I would put China in that basket, to democracy, they move in their own way and based on the culture of their nation and the personalities of the leaders who could make that change. So, for example, in Russia, Putin brought in an authoritarian form of democracy, and it still is. It had to be that way, because you couldn't shift from the Communism that was in the USSR to full democracy; it was impossible. It's an evolutionary concept.

My prediction is this: As incomes in China increases to around $10,000 to $15,000, which we're quite a way away from, yet, what will happen is, people will demand more freedom. In demanding freedom, they will demand democracy. For me, it is absolutely inevitable that China will open up to more democratic forms of governance. It will be unable to suppress the people's growth needs. Just exactly the same as happened in Egypt and Tunisia, and is happening in Syria right now. You cannot stop the evolution of individuals. Once they've got their deficiency needs met, they will want to meet their growth needs. What that means is, they will want to individuate and self-actualize, and they will want freedom. Not just freedom of expression, but freedom from fear. That, for me, is critical. That's the movement.

When I watched what was happening in Egypt a year or so ago, and I heard people in the streets so joyful, what I noticed was, I didn't hear anybody saying, "Oh I'm so joyful because now I can have a government I can vote for." No, what I heard them saying was, "We have freedom from fear." That's why I call my book, *Love, Fear, and the Destiny of Nations*, because fear plays a huge part in human evolution.

China, in terms of the people who live there, is no different from anywhere else on the planet. China will become democratic within the next 20 years. Absolutely. Can't be avoided.

Will it be formal democracy, we don't know. It will be somewhere on that scale. It won't be a liberal democracy, but it will be a more electoral democracy, where people can actually vote. Electoral democracy is not that much different from authoritarian regime, but at least it's progressing down the path.

**Nicholas:** You just slipped that one in.

**Richard:** Yes, but they have to go at their own speed. It's like when Bush went into Iraq and said, "We're going to bring democracy to Iraq." What? Here are three tribes: the Kurds, Sunnis, and the Shiites, who all have different belief systems, who are operating in the deficiency need area. They're not ready for democracy. Democracy's a values-based process. You've got to get past your beliefs. People cling together with their beliefs, in their communities, in order to survive. Once they can survive, then they can move into a values-driven framework, which is democracy. So it's taking a while for it to happen in Iraq. It'll take a while for it to happen anywhere where people are struggling to meet their needs.

**Nicholas:** You mentioned that, for democracy to happen, people's lower-level needs need to be in place first, like food, security, etc. That makes sense. Is there anything else? What are the conditions required for democracy to evolve or occur?

**Richard:** In Part II of *Love, Fear, and the Destiny of Nations*, I talk about the democracy journey and the stages. I label these stages with values. For democracy to flourish, you first of all have to have freedom. It begins with freedom. What that means is freedom for the masses to be able to live their lives no longer under the duress of the elites. The big issue there in freedom is the difference between masses and elites.

What's so interesting is, democracy move so slowly because the people who govern are the elites, and they become new elites. Even now, in the UK, we have an elitist government. Same in America. It's almost like you become a member of the government, you get elected, and you enter into the new elite. Where democracy works best is where the differences in inequality are least. For example, leading the way are the Nordic nations, where there is very little inequality. An elitism is practically nonexistent.

First of all, democracy is a shift away from elitism, basically. So the first one is freedom.

Second, once you've got freedom, comes equality. We had a democracy in the UK, and other countries did, but we didn't have equality, because women couldn't vote until the 1920s. So then comes equality. After equality, not comes accountability.

Freedom, equality, accountability. Once we've got those in place, we can move forward into fairness, openness, transparency, and, finally, trust. Trust is the highest order value that we need to be able to live in a liberal democracy.

**Nicholas:** Richard, what I'd really like to do, if you'd be so kind, is to run through each of those very powerful values, and describe what it looks like when it's operating at its best.

**Richard:** Let's take freedom, for a start. When it's operating at its best, the people in the nation have freedom from fear. Not only do they have freedom of expression, but because they've got freedom of expression, because they can express themselves, the reason they can express themselves, is because they have no more fear. When people have that sense of being able to say whatever it is, not to slander people, but to be able to express who they are and their thought, that's what freedom looks like. It's ultimately about freedom from fear.

Equality. We have gender equality, which is vitally important. When you get to the concept of a nation, sometimes you have different ethnic groups making up that nation. If you look at the Nordic countries, it's very homogeneous, so they may have been able to make big advances in equality, because they've not had ethnic differences. When you start introducing people from other cultures in significantly large numbers, now equality has a new challenge. For example, in the USA, with all of the people who came over from Africa. There was a huge movement in America, to get Black equality. It's easier when it's homogeneous; it's not so easy when you've got very many different cultures.

That's one thing to be said, I think, about the USA, is that it's a huge experiment in equality. Forget the income inequality; I'll deal with that in a moment. In terms of racial equality. It's a huge. There's Hispanics, there's Asians, there's African-Americans. It's like a melting pot of cultures and religions. Getting to equality in that situation is much more difficult than in Sweden, for example.

Now comes to the other aspect. I've talked about gender equality or racial equality, but income equality. When you get income equality, it improves every aspect to the way that a nation functions, all the way from teenage pregnancies to number of people in prisons. By creating income equality, you begin to build trust. That's the key to the income equality piece. Equality, three different dimensions: racial, gender, and income.

Next comes to accountability. This might sound like a bit of a hobby horse but I guess I get very upset by the way that the UK and the USA are governed, because we have these, basically, two-party politics. Two-party politics, when you look at it closely, is simply a throwback to the times when we had the rich elites and the poor masses. What we've got now, we've got a middle class aspiring to be the rich elites, who may vote Conservative or Republican, but for me, two-party politics is a recipe for no accountability, because they're always blaming each other. If something goes wrong, the other one blames the other one, and then they take over and try to do better, and it's all the past government's fault the way that things are right now.

**Nicholas:** I'd agree that it's highly immature, because of the way the people operate within it, but they would argue the opposite. They would argue that, say, David Cameron, our Prime Minister, having to stand up and be critically cross-examined by a jeering mob, although it doesn't lead to high-level sophisticated discussions, it does mean there's accountability in a way that ...

**Richard:** I don't see it, and nobody else in the country sees it, either. Because when you look at the measures of accountability that people see in their government, it's in terms of freedom, equality, accountability, openness, fairness, transparency, and trust, it's still appalling. I don't see accountability. The expenses scandal in the UK was an absolute travesty of accountability, personal accountability of elected people. I don't see this accountability.

**Nicholas:** So this might be ...

**Richard:** At the personal level of our elected leaders.

**Nicholas:** But some people would say the consensus-based coalition-type governments encourage cosy deals behind closed doors, and so on, whereas a much more vigorous, aggressive debate ...

**Richard:** I don't see that. I think the contrary is absolutely true. I think the contrary to that is absolutely true. You see, I've listened to David Cameron. When we had that vote to go for the new voting system, and he said, "No, we don't want consensus. We want to be able to make decisions." "David Cameron," I said to myself, "everything in the UK is either black or white; it's either Labour or Conservative." Frankly, I love lots of shades of gray. I want to be able to choose the shade of gray that

I vote for. I don't want somebody in power who, once they're in power, feels they can do whatever they want because they've got the majority. I don't want that. I want people to build consensus so we've got multiple shades of gray in the way that we're governed.

David Cameron and the other leaders that support the way that we're governed right now, they support it because they become the new elites. It serves their ego to be a new elite. Right now, this vote coming up on transparency. It's about what can be disclosed in a court by spies. The argument is, "No, we don't want transparency, because we need to protect that information." To me, that is not democracy. We elected you to govern on our behalf. We want to know what the hell's going on.

**Nicholas:** What steps, what practical steps, do you think could Britain and America and the other Western countries take to make a step forward, to improve the level of accountability.

**Richard:** First of all, I'm sad to say, we need some new leaders. We've got an old leadership paradigm in place, which comes from self-esteem consciousness. It's all about the self-interest of the individual. I know there are many people in government who go there to make a difference, but once you start climbing up the ladder of politics, it becomes self-interest. Once you want to become a minister, it becomes ego, it becomes status, it becomes self-interest.

We know these people are operating out of the lower levels of consciousness. We want people operating out of the higher levels of consciousness. The whole system is built around that. For example, spin doctors. They're constantly protecting the ego, or protecting the people in power, by putting a different spin. What's that about? We need openness. We don't need it hiding behind closed doors. I'm all for accountability. I'm into the openness and transparency piece right now. What can we do to make more people more accountable?

I'll tell you one thing we could do. There could be, by necessity, everybody who stands for election or is elected, does a leadership course about leading self, about moral responsibility, about the common good, about what they're being asked to do for you and me, for the general public. A leadership course that puts it really clearly that this isn't about their self-esteem; this is about the common good of the people. I would love to see such a leadership course for everybody who becomes a politician. Make it even a pre-requirement to even stand for election.

**Nicholas:** Presumably, for that to be authentic, people need to already be at that state to be able to rise to the stage ...

**Richard:** No, they need to be willing. They need to be willing to embrace that.

**Nicholas:** But if someone who's at the egocentric stage or ...

**Richard:** Then they probably wouldn't make it through the course.

**Nicholas:** I see, yes. Fair enough. (LAUGHTER)

**Richard:** Now who decides who makes it or not? That's the big question. I don't even want to go there. What I'm saying, my main point is, we need a new leadership paradigm from "I" to "we," from "What's in it for me?" to "What's best for the common good?" from "Being the best in the world" to "The best for the world." We need that. We need higher-thinking people.

**Nicholas:** Like you, I've met many politicians, and find that, privately, I've never met one who didn't genuinely want to make the world a better place.

**Richard:** Right.

**Nicholas:** Of course, they've got egos and they've got shadow sides and dark sides and there's dirty pragmatism and so on. They seem broadly genuine. But what I've noticed is that, we say we want this new level of leader, which would be wonderful, but of course, the followers matter and the media matter. Part of the reason I didn't go into politics at a much earlier stage was because I just thought I would be eaten by a bunch of piranha, essentially, if you're an authentic person. For example, the fiction that everybody in the Cabinet agrees with each other on everything. It's completely ridiculous, that's totally stupid. But ...

**Richard:** Here's what I would like to say to you. I really fully understand that argument. You know, the leaders you get represent the average level of consciousness of the nation. So you get the leaders you deserve. Expand your question a bit to, "What can we do?" Well, what we can do is alleviate poverty, minimize inequality, so the masses can individuate and self-actualize. That's really about the evolution of human consciousness. If we can do that in a nation, we will gradually get better and better leaders.

In some ways, there's not much you can do if people always elect the people to represent them who will represent their average level of consciousness. That's it. So what we need to do is lift the average level of consciousness of the nation. We do that by minimizing inequality, by helping people grow and develop, and being able to meet their deficiency needs. I think that's what we see in the Scandinavian, or the Nordic, countries. That's what we see. Guess what? They've got coalition governments, because they've got multiple shades of gray, because people have informed decisions, now. They've individuated the self-actualized. They have an opinion, which is an educated opinion, about how things should be.

**Nicholas:** What comes after accountability in the evolutionary development?

**Richard:** We start with freedom, equality, accountability, fairness. Fairness is all about being able to show that equality is happening in every system, process of governance of the people. Again, you'll see that what it does is that it minimizes elitism. By having more fairness, you reduce the possibility of elitism, because the elites are treated exactly the same way as the masses are. Once people get into power, fairness can sometimes be a problem.

Fairness is an interesting one, because, in a sense, fairness is the basis of justice. If you go back and look, from an evolutionary standpoint, let's go back three or four hundred years, where we had Kings and Queens. If you were to define "fairness" in that, fairness was quite different, and justice was quite different. If you stole a sheep, you were hung, drawn, and quartered, and that was the end of it. There were, I believe, over two hundred crimes you could commit which had the death penalty, and around the late 1700s it went down from two hundred some to four, the crimes you could commit that would have the death penalty. Suddenly there was a sort of an enlightenment about this.

What did justice look like, and fairness look like, in that previous period? The point of justice and fairness in that previous period was to maintain the internal stability of the nation, because it was ruled by elites. In order to maintain the internal stability, they had to have severe punishment. As elitism began to disappear and we began to have forms of democracy, so justice changed and the principles of justice changed, to fairness.

I believe there's a future evolution of justice. You can begin to see it happening. It's about moral integrity. Justice will be looked at through the eyes of moral integrity; not just fairness, but moral integrity.

**Nicholas:** What do you mean by that, Richard. Could you give an example?

**Richard:** Yes. The MP's expenses scandal in the UK. They didn't do anything wrong, but they set up rules which, if somebody independent had looked at it and said, "Wait a minute, you're benefiting from your position. There's no moral integrity here around fairness." Moral integrity will, I think, become one of the new platforms for justice.

You see it already happening. I think, in the last years, there have been at least three ministers in the UK government who handed in their notice or got fired over issues of moral integrity. Plain and simple. You see it. We're becoming more and more values driven. When people breach the common, human, positive values that we demand from the people who we ask to govern us, they're gone.

**Nicholas:** I definitely agree with that and observe that. One of the problems with that, one of the challenges with that, is that people are not very honest. I don't mean the people who do the overt cheating or the fiddling; I mean the people who are doing the judging. None of us are perfect. We might say, "Oh, we want love, peace, joy, and harmony," but you might want a lot of darker things: lust, sex, competition, money, power, control, and all the wounded side and the fear-based side plays out. And people are not very honest about that. So when it comes to poor old politicians, they get held up by this holier-than-thou, they've got to be Jesus, Gandhi, etc. How can we be more ...

**Richard:** Who is there that can honestly throw a stone because we haven't had some infidelity or something that in the past? Nobody. But we all grow and evolve. What happens is, you grow past it because it doesn't work for you. You begin to realize that this shadow side doesn't work for you. This is what I call, "Leading self." It's about personal mastery. It's part of the evolution of the human individual. This is why I come back to leadership development. This isn't about leading people; it starts with leading self, moral integrity. My point, here, is that it's okay to have a shadow past. It's not okay to have a shadow present.

**Nicholas:** 99% of people do.

**Richard:** If I did something a long time ago, I can ask for forgiveness; I can say, "You know what? I can admit now that that was wrong. I don't see it that way. Okay. That's in my past. I'm past that. This is how I live now." If in the now you are living these indiscretions and you've been elected by people, that's not okay with me.

**Nicholas:** Is there not a way we could be more mature about it? If you go back to medieval times, with witch burning of the ones who contained the evil and they had to be destroyed; where in Victorian times, or today the Taliban, or Islamic fundamentalists, if someone breaks the rule and all hell breaks loose and they're absolutely crucified. Of course, people are very happily, smugly projecting their own dark side onto that person who gets killed and takes the responsibility for it. Could we not be a bit more compassionate about our leaders and say, "You don't have to be perfect?" Because if our leaders all have to be Jesus and Buddha rolled into one, the only people who are going to do it are going to be psychopaths and narcissists who think that ...

**Richard:** I think that you're misunderstanding what I'm saying here. All I'm saying is coming back to the word that you used, which is "honesty."

I notice, actually, there are several things about the present government that I like. When something has come up that has been non-transparent or non-open and it's become public, David Cameron has acted immediately. In a sense, it's an inheritance from the past, this way of being. I'm not asking for people to be pure Buddhas or Jesus. I'm simply asking them to realize and to work on their moral integrity as part of being a leader.

This is what I do in the business world. This is how I make my money in the business world. We map values and we help leaders evolve and grow. All I'm saying is, there is not much focus on that in the leaders of our nation and in the leaders of our communities. There's no focus on how do you grow and develop as a leader. It's not even on the agenda, hardly. If I'm committing to be a leader, I need to commit to my own leadership improvement.

In the business world, when I wrote *Liberating the Corporate Soul* in 1996, I had three mantras. First of all, cultural capitalism, new frontier, competitive advantage. Who you are as an organization will be really important for your success. Secondly, cultural transformation, creating that culture, begins with the personal transformation of the leaders, because the culture of the organization is a reflection of their leadership consciousness. As they shift their consciousness and their values, the culture changes, and the success of the company changes. We've got so much evidence for that right now. But I don't see that happening in the political sphere. I don't see it. That's what I'm saying: Our leaders need to be more accountable for their own personal growth and development.

**Nicholas:** From your experience in the business world, obviously there are some areas of business where people support what you're talking about, and other areas where they're prehistoric. Can you encourage people to take that path? Or do you have to wait until they're ready and they choose to do it?

**Richard:** Both. If they're not willing to look at themselves, then don't even worry about it; you're not going to get anywhere. Business leaders watch what other people are doing. They say, "What's he doing" or "What's she doing that's making them so successful? Oh, they're building a values-driven company. Oh, they're putting resources into making a better world. They've got a higher vision for the company than simply being the number-one supplier of." It's almost as if, in business, there's a self-correcting mechanism that says, "Aha. As these companies, consciously led, become more and more successful" and, by the way, there's a lot of data on the conscious capitalism movement that shows you that conscious capitalism pays off amazingly, in terms of the bottom line.

What is conscious capitalism? It's built on three pillars. It's built on a higher purpose, other than making money. It's built on equal consideration to all stakeholders. It's employees, customers, shareholders, local community, and society. And it's built on conscious leadership and conscious culture. These are the four conditions; basically, it's values driven.

If you read a book called *Firms of Endearment*, you'll see how amazing the results are from these companies. In fact, just four weeks ago, I was in California with some of the leaders, seven or eight of the CEOs or the leaders of this movement and a number of thought leaders, for four days, talking about this movement and how it has been so successful, from an economic standpoint. There were venture capitalists there who were saying, "This is it. This is what we've been looking for." Because not only does it create, it creates wellbeing for everybody. Everybody is considered and everybody. It's a win, win, win, win, win, win, win, win situation for everybody, as a society as well as shareholders as well as customers, as well as employees.

This is a new paradigm of thinking for me. This is what it's about. I don't see that happening in politics. All I see is lots egos, people being ego-driven but also saying, "I want to make a difference." Sometimes their egos, the shadow side that you mentioned, gets in the way. I'm saying, "Oh, okay. If you really want to make a difference, think a little about how you're undermining yourself by allowing your ego motivations to shoot yourself in the foot. Because that's what's happening to you."

My point really is, that I'm not asking for all our leaders to be perfect, to be stainless. No, all I want is them to recognize that they can improve who they are by not just only focusing on make a difference, but also on learning to lead themselves, getting their egos out of the way, so they can actually live equality, fairness, and accountability, openness, and transparency, and trust. Because that's what will happen once their egos get out of the way. They become more authentic individuals. They become more appreciated by the public. The moral integrity improves and everybody says, "Wow."

Look at the great leaders. Look at the great leaders. They had moral integrity: Nelson Mandela, Gandhi. Moral integrity is what they stood for.

**Nicholas:** Could you say a little bit about the last step, transparency?

**Richard:** Yes. The faster we get to accountability, fairness, openness. Now, openness is about being willing to disclose your motivations for doing things. So when I have a conversation with you, I say, "Look, you know, the reason I'm making this suggestion is because ..." And I'm authentic and open about it, and I'm willing to listen to what you have to say.

Openness is difficult because, in our present systems of government in most of the leading nations, not all of them, it's about debate. You put your point of view. I listen to what you're saying, not to appreciate it, but to shoot it down.

Now, I don't listen with the way of thinking, "Aha, we have a dialogue here. That, actually, is a good point. I could incorporate that into what I'm thinking." No, we don't do that. We're built on this old idea of dog-eat-dog debate. I attack you, you attack me, and nobody listens. All I'm listening for is your flaws so I can get my point of view across. In that situation, you're not willing to be open, because you'll get destroyed, and that's the reason you gave earlier about not wanting to go into politics: You don't want to get destroyed.

To live openness means having the moral integrity to disclose your motivations to people, and being willing to say, "This is where I am and I am not sure about that. But this I am sure about, because of this, this, and this." It's about declaring who you are in a way which exposes. And you become defenseless, in a way. But there's a power in defenselessness. There's a power in openness, which you don't get when you're closed. Because when you're open, people get it at a different level; they understand you at a different level. Our system's not set up that way, so we don't get a lot of openness.

Then transparency is slightly different from openness, because transparency is about the willingness, not to declare your motivations, but to have every system or procedure open to scrutiny, have all the documentation open to scrutiny. Julian Assange, he's onto something huge. He's heavily criticized, but I think he's onto something huge. Because when you and I elect some people to represent us, we want an openness and we want transparency. We don't want these to become the new elite, and that's what, exactly, happens: They become the new elite.

You and I don't participate in democracy. Well, we do: for 10 minutes every four years, when we vote. That's the only way you and I participate in democracy. For me, that's not good enough. I don't want that type of democracy where I participate for 10 minutes every four years. I want to be able to influence the person who represents me, and to have the ability for that person to influence the government, not in debate, but in dialog. It's a whole new way of being. I teach that in the leadership teams. I teach people how to listen. I call it, "Circle Time," where everybody gets to state their point of view and nobody gets to interrupt except to ask for clarity. You go around once or twice. What happens is, people begin to shift their positions as they listen, to appreciate rather than listening to destroy, which is what happens in debates in parliamentary proceedings.

It's so old-fashioned. Nicholas, it's old-fashioned. We want to move beyond this. We're so much better than this. We deserve so much better than what we've got.

Openness. Transparency. Finally, when all these values are in place, you can get trust. Where is the highest level of trust? The Nordic countries. Who's at the bottom of the scale in Europe? UK and the USA. Really low levels of trust. Absolutely low levels of trust. We don't trust our politicians. We don't even trust each other, because of the inequality. The present government isn't that much interested in my opinion, in reducing the inequalities, because they're so much in the pockets of the rich elites. And the rich elites don't want equality; they want inequality, because they want to line their pockets.

In the USA and the UK, we don't really have democracy, because in the US, policymaking is heavily influenced by rich, powerful corporations, and in the UK is influenced elites of the establishment, House of Lords. Nobody elected these people. They represent the establishment. They represent rich elites. They don't represent the people. This is not democracy. We do not have democracy in the UK, in my opinion. It's ranked number 18 or 19th in the democracy scale by the Economic Intelligence Unit. I think it's ranked 17th and the US is 19th, or vice versa. We're way down the democracy scale. France just got moved from "full democracy" into "flawed democracy," and so did Italy. Why? Because of their leaders: Sarkozy and Berlusconi. Operating out of ego-consciousness. Sarkozy, I understand, has 110 cars underneath the Elysee Palace, and according to some newspaper reports, he spends 10,000 pounds a day on food at the Elysee. It's like the new elitism. It means, "If I can get elected, I become part of the elite."

**Nicholas:** Can you give an example, from your experience, where trust is working really well. It's up and running and what does it look like?

**Richard:** Scandinavia. Sweden. Look at the data there. It works brilliantly. People in Scandinavia enjoy paying their taxes, because they all get so much out of it. Their children get so much out of it. Greece is exactly the polar opposite. Even the politicians in Greece want to avoid paying taxes. That's why the country's in such a mess. They've got all the tax laws in place but nobody collects. You pay a bribe and you don't pay any taxes. Greece and Sweden are opposite ends of the spectrum.

Now, they've got a lot of advantages. They've got this homogeneous population. They've got this level of trust. It's so much higher. I've got data in my book about all of these points. High-trust democracy turns out to be the best in terms of human development index, it turns out to be the best in terms of just about any indicator that you can think of. High-trust nations turn out to be the best.

Well, there we are. We've done freedom, accountability, equality, fairness, openness, transparency, and trust.

**Nicholas:** Fantastic.

**Richard:** You know, this is all happening right in front of us. I love it. I love reading the newspapers every day and see all this lack of moral integrity popping up, and people getting fired, and thinking, "When are we going to learn? When are the people in power going to learn, it's about moral integrity?"

**Nicholas:** Could you say a bit about how love and fear play out in the destiny of nations and the evolution of consciousness?

**Richard:** Sure. What I do in this book is, I demonstrate that, basically, it's these basic human emotions that influence world affairs. "Love" is a synonym, for me, for "attraction," and "fear" is a synonym for "separation" or "rejection." Attraction/rejection. Repulsion, basically. You see it through an atomic level, and the cellular level, and we see it, also, with *Homo sapiens*.

It turns out that, in order to become viable independent and then bond to form group structures, you have to get past fear and embrace trust in order to form those group structures. If you were to have a scale of deep fear all the way to high love, trust would be right in the middle; neutral. When you were born, or when I was born, we were born with trust, because, as babies, there was nothing else we could do. We were totally dependent on those around us. And we learned from that experience, to trust or not trust our parents, our siblings, and the culture in which we live. We learned some fear-based beliefs, if we were not actually brought up by self-actualized parents who really understood who we were. And if we were, then what happened was we grew up with very few subconscious fears.

What we see in the world right now is a lot of young people coming along, operating at what I think is high levels of consciousness. Why? Because they were brought up by parents who managed satisfy their deficiency needs, had sufficient income to do that, and so brought up their children in a self-actualized way. So these children were brought up without all of these cultural beliefs and personal beliefs that they had deficiencies. This is a hope for the future. Because the more parents are self-actualized, the more they bring up self-actualized children, who bring up more self-actualized children.

Basically, one of the things in the book is that, ultimately, everything happens at an energetic level, at the quantum level of existence, if you like, fear is a very heavy energy, and what happens is that it stresses us, it holds us back, we feel it. When we've been in a stressful day, we just want to sit down and have a drink and lighten up. Whereas love, on the other hand, is a very light energy, and it's a very expressive energy. And trust lies neutral, right in the middle.

What I'm saying is that love and fear influence how we're growing and evolving, both individually and in nations. I haven't mentioned this yet, the Seven Levels of Consciousness model, which fits with many other models about personal growth and development, survival, relationship, self-esteem. You could put it like surviving, conforming in order to belong, differentiating yourself to build your self-esteem, individuating as you break out of everything you learned. We're all conditioned during our childhood by our parents and our culture. Individuation is a midpoint where you begin to break out of that and transform. And then you move into the higher levels, where you begin to want to find out who you really are and what gift you can bring to the world. Like you doing this series: This is a gift that you're bringing to the world. Why are you doing it? Well, you don't really know, because it's coming from deep within you, as my work comes from deep within me. It's who you are, as a soul.

What happens is, as you actualize this sense of meaning, you make a difference in the world, and that's what you're trying to do. That's what everybody's trying to do. You're trying to make a difference in the world. Then, when you get into that point of making a difference and it becomes a way of life, you basically want to serve. It's the only thing you want to do.

So the Seven Levels of Consciousness are aligned with the three universal stages of evolution, stuff that's explained in the book. But, what I'm really saying here is that love and trust and fear forms a continuum. As we can shift the masses out of fear, out of their deficiency needs, to move up to trust, to move up to want to, then, naturally, satisfy their growth needs, we create the survival conditions to make that happen, we live in a better world.

**Nicholas:** Something I've noticed in my experience is that a lot of people coming from a very Christian perspective or a New Age way of thinking, or even just someone who is, in our country, a *Guardian* reader, someone who considers themselves quite liberal, they will often say, "Oh, it's really important to come from a place of love and possibility and potential." And who could disagree with that? A lot of those people will look upon the *Daily Mail* reader, or the Fox News viewer, for the Americans, and have a lot of contempt for them and say, "They're bad. They're coming from a place of fear. They're all about worrying about crime and immigration and unemployment and so on." It's all disaster, disaster, disaster, and so on. Obviously, there are really good arguments for one should want to be a positive and optimistic person. But also, it is appropriate to be attuned to real threats, isn't it?

It's very easy for people who grow up in a nice, safe place to a nice family which are prosperous and live in an area where everyone around them is like they are, and they don't have to worry about crime, they don't have to worry about poverty or anything at all. For them, it totally is easy to live in this place of love, or at least apparent love.

**Richard:** Until a disaster happens, or until something happens in their lives, where they drop down into fear, because they haven't mastered fear?

**Nicholas:** Yes. Plus, if those people are all in leadership positions, then you could argue that, if everyone is operating at that level of consciousness at the leadership level, then they can create systems which don't account for behaviors at the bottom level. I was watching a David Attenborough program about emperor penguins building their nests the other day. There was a very funny, but also very sad thing, where one penguin was going to ...

**Richard:** I saw it.

**Nicholas:** He was collecting stones to build his nest and another one was watching him and when the first penguin went off to get a new stone, the other would steal a stone from his nest. It was really funny to watch, because it was so cheeky. But, of course, humans are like that, too. Some people aren't like that, but there will always be queue jump-ers, there'll always be people who'll want to cheat, who want to pull a fast one, who want the quick fix, and so on. If we only come from a place of naïveté, if coming from a place of love means naïveté, then that's not going to work, because the darkness, the evil will come through.

**Richard:** For me, there's graduations in everything. There's graduations in love. That's why the Seven Levels of Consciousness model is so inter-esting and helpful. The people you're describing here, who are coming from love but can find it in themselves to judge people who are not, are not highly evolved. A researcher at Keegan has a three-part model which links very closely to the three universal stages of evolution. He basically says the people at the bottom end are the socialized mind. They try to fit in and that's all they try to do. That, in my 7 stage system, is the first three levels of consciousness.

Then comes the self-authoring mind-people who manage to get past all their socialization and are doing well in the world and know what they want and go out there and get it. This is the sort of people that you're talking about here. There's an increasing number of people moving into that category. But what happens with the self-authoring mind is that they see the world through their belief structure. They can't see the world through other people's belief structures.

Until you move to the third stage, which is the self-transforming mind. The self-transforming mind doesn't see the world, doesn't necessarily operate in the world through its own belief structure, but is willing and can listen to other ideas, and accommodate them and transform, and understands that there are multiple levels of consciousness and that people are growing and evolving. So Fox News applies to the socialized mind. It applies to those people, and that's okay. It's okay. You don't have to judge it; it's what is. Then another level of evolution will watch a dif-ferent news.

I don't think there's anything really out there for the self-transforming mind right yet, because there are just a few percent of the people live in that space, who are able to see this evolutionary perspective in terms of what they see around them, and the values that are lived in the people that are around them. For most people, what they see is flat land, and they judge themselves based on other people. If you're still judging yourself, "In order to feel good I have to put these people down," that is not evolved. Some of these people who embrace love, they go, "So how long did you meditate today? I meditated for an hour." It's pure self-esteem consciousness at level three, with a spiritual twist. But it's still the lower deficiency needs and the need to look better. All this spiritual approach and this love and Kumbaya, etc. breeds its own hierarchy, and you've got to get beyond that.

When I wrote *New Leadership Paradigm*, I didn't want to write a book on leadership, and I thought, "Well, what have I got to offer, because there's 300,000 titles on leadership?" What I realized was, everybody writes about leadership on the levels of consciousness at which they operate. So Donald Trump, on leadership, represents a certain level of consciousness. Jack Welsh on leadership, slightly higher, but a different level of consciousness. And so on. What I realized was, there was nobody writing about leadership from the full spectrum. In other words, from all Seven Levels of Consciousness, from the lowest to the highest. And those low levels are important. You need to have a positive way to survive. You need to have positive relationships. And you need a positive sense of self-esteem.

But that's the domain of the ego, so you can also have limiting values at those three levels, fears that drag you down. So the answer to that question is simply, "It's okay. You just have to realize that the world is passing through evolution, that people are passing through evolution." And you have to go and say, "Oh, that's where they are," and not judge it.

**Nicholas:** To give a really meaty practical example, and also for one of the most hot-potato subjects, how would you design an immigration policy from that top level of consciousness, from the self-transforming consciousness?

**Richard:** An immigration policy. You know, that is a really complex problem. No matter whether you're an atom, a cell, a human being, or a nation, whatever you are, you have to maintain internal stability and external equilibrium. If you're out of internal stability and external equilibrium, you've got problems. It applies to a nation; it applies to governments.

For me, the whole question of this immigration policy gets to the point: how does this policy help us maintain internal stability and external equilibrium? Because, as a nation, we can grow and develop if we have internal stability and external equilibrium. If we throw out the balance by having a policy that creates separation, inequality, we're going to create more internal instability. For me, the criteria, is how do we maximize internal stability and external equilibrium?

How you do that depends on where you are on your levels of consciousness. For example, if you've got a nation where there are a lot of masses trying to meet their deficiency needs and you bring in an open-doors immigration policy that brings in more poor people who, then, compete for these lower jobs where you've got a lot of people already competing, you're going to get more internal instability. However, you live in a nation like Iceland, for example, where everybody's really quite ... I won't say they're evolved, because they're not. They had a complete financial crash because of some level-one and level-three issues, survival and self-esteem issues, which they allowed to get out of hand. But where you've got a larger proportion of the people who are operating at higher levels of consciousness, then you can have a different policy than if you're in a different nation, where the levels of consciousness are different.

If one of the things about *Love, Fear, and the Destiny of Nations* is Volume One. There's Volume Two. And Volume Two is about how we've been measuring the consciousness of nations, 15 nations; by the end of this year it'll be 20 nations. But we've actually measured the consciousness.

For me, designing an immigration policy is about understanding internal stability and external equilibrium and matching the policy to where people are in the nation. There is not one solution fits all. A solution in Sweden will be different to a solution in UK, which will be different to a solution in USA.

**Nicholas:** In our country, and in similar countries, the debate on that subject would normally be between the liberal and the conservative positions, which, I think, you would call was at the socialized level of consciousness and the ...

**Richard:** The socialized mind and the self-authoring mind.

**Nicholas:** The people who have been most successful in making immigration policy over the last 50 years, have been the people at the liberal level. But they're, of course, the people at the level that you talk about, the flat-lands, the level of relativism and everyone being sensitive and equal and they don't even understand that the people lower in level of consciousness from them are still operating at a rather more primitive level. Therefore, the immigration policies they pursue are quite dangerous and do disrupt the equilibrium, in the way that you describe, in a number of ways, because they import large numbers of people operating at a lower level of consciousness and behavior, and those people will go and live in places where people, already here, operating at lower levels of consciousness, live. And there's a lot of conflict there and a lot of problems. Of course, the nice, liberal people don't live in those places and don't experience it. So when they hear the local people squeal about it and say, "What the hell are you doing?" they just call them "racists" and throw abuse at them.

Anyway, punch line is, question is: What can we do to encourage, cata-lyze the people at the liberal, self-authoring level of consciousness, step up to that higher, integral, transformative level of consciousness, so they actually get it, so they take responsibility for all levels of consciousness?

**Richard:** It comes to my whole point about leadership and leading yourself. Leadership begins with leading yourself. Any individual. The *New Leadership Paradigm* book that I wrote, and the learning system that goes with it, I made it available on the web. I wanted to democratize leadership development, so you can download the "Leading Self," "Lead-ing your Team," "Leading your Organization." You can download these for $30. Because leadership development, right now, is the privilege of the elites. The very rich elites or the very top of the people in the com-pany. I think leadership development, in terms of leading the self, should be available to everybody on the planet, if they wanted it.

The natural process by which one's people have begun to satisfy their deficiency needs at the survival, relationship, and self-esteem level, they want to explore these higher levels of consciousness. They want to move forward. And as they begin to individuate, the let go of the conditioning and they begin to operate in the self-authoring mind. But then, naturally, they will move towards the self-transforming mind. So what are the conditions?

First of all, we have to be able to satisfy people's deficiency needs, and then we have to be able to encourage people to explore their growth needs. What that looks like, I'm not sure. It is a natural progression for people in their personal evolution.

It has a lot to do with education, and education at two levels. First of all, the education that we get in our schools, which is not geared, it doesn't have this flatland thing and it's based more on intellect than emotion or even spirituality. It's not geared to moving people up through these levels of consciousness. It's just based on intellect and getting a job, basically. So that education system would need a vast overhaul in order for children to be able to get in touch with what they're good at, what they're passionate about, and explore that. At the same time, be able to learn the skills to meet their deficiency needs; in other words, get a job. We could do a lot in education.

The other part of that is, education at home, emotional education. Parents who are not evolved will judge their children. Children will find it difficult to find pleasure and avoid pain because they're living in a dysfunctional environment. In some respect, every family's dysfunctional. When you're operating out of the lower levels of consciousness, where you've got a lot of needs and stress, your children will be brought up in an atmosphere of negative beliefs and negative assumptions, and they'll have to grow out of that throughout their lives. That's where they start. Parental education, or helping parents understand who they are and how they bring up their children, and changing the education system so that it's full-spectrum consciousness, in other words, it deals with children at every level, at what they're good at, at the emotional level, and I said, "Spiritual level," but more for me it's, "What are you passionate about? What do you enjoy doing as a kid? Let's have you do more of that? Let's explore your creativity." Because our present system takes creativity out of children. If you can stay in touch with your creativity, you've got a better chance of self-actualizing than if you don't.

**Nicholas:** That's a brilliant place to end.

Richard, obviously the big-picture question here is, "What's the state of Western Civilization? Where are we going? What's the future?" Is there any area that you haven't commented on that you'd like to?

**Richard:** I just wanted to say that the most important thing I would stress is stop looking at the world from flatland. See it as an evolutionary process. Right now, I would say the one thing I would like to stress is that what's happening in the European Union, for me, is a potential model for regional governance, and it's at the cutting edge of evolution. Even in the present crisis of sovereign debt, what's happening is they're finding ways to solve that problem. Evolution happens by trying this and it doesn't work, and then we try that; but there's a pattern to it. Stop looking at the world from Flatland and begin to understand, it's all evolution that's going on, personally and societally. See through those eyes rather than this judgmental flatland. That's my big message. It's all happening in front of our eyes. It's fascinating. It's fantastic. It's amazing. We're all doing what we came to do: That's grow and learn and evolve. Man, at the individual and at the societal level. Wow, what a program.

**Nicholas:** One last thing. Can I ask you a techie question?

**Richard:** Sure.

**Nicholas:** I'm quite familiar with the Spiral Dynamics and Integral models, and I know from your books that you've obviously read those. Is there anything very different in your system to those, or is it pretty much the same thing?

**Richard:** It's similar and different. The Spiral Dynamics model maps to the seven levels of consciousness in a very relatively easy way. For example, the Beige represents the survival. The Purple represents relationship, level two. Then what happens is, the power, the authority, and the status, the Red, Blue, and Orange, all slot into self-esteem consciousness, level three. Thereafter, it follows pretty much the simple one-for-one plan.

It's very similar. A lot of these models are very, very similar. I'm not saying one is better than the other. The advantage that we have found with the Seven Levels model is that we can use it to measure consciousness, in a very detailed way, by mapping values. Because every value that you express links to a level of consciousness. By simply asking people in organizations and nations, "What are your personal values? Pick 10 from the list. Customize. What values represent how your organization or nation operates? What represent how you'd like it to operate? Pick 10." You accumulate that. You have a really detailed map of the consciousness of the nation, and what is working and what is not working and what people want.

That's what happened in Iceland. We mapped the values of Iceland just before it crashed. I went there two weeks before and said, "You've got leadership issues. If you were an organization, you'd be going bankrupt about now." They did. We can map consciousness. We can map where people are and what they want. In any particular nation, it will be different. Being able to do that makes the evolution of consciousness conscious at an organizational and at a national level.

**Nicholas:** If anyone would like to follow your work or make contact with you, what web address would you recommend?

**Richard:** You can go to valuescentre.com, and then look at my name, Richard Barrett, or you can get to the same place by doing RichardBarrett.net. It'll take you to the same place. On that page, there's everything that I'm up to: videos, blogs, books, etc., etc.

**Nicholas:** Fantastic. Thank you so much for your time, Richard. It's been an enormous pleasure I think I could talk to you for twice as long. Enormous pleasure talking to you. Thank you, very much.

**Richard:** Good. Thanks, Nicholas. Bye.

# Resurrecting Christianity

## Rising to the Challenges of a Complex World

**Bishop Michael Nazir-Ali interviewed by Dr Nicholas Beecroft**
Bishop Michael Nazir-Ali was the 106th Bishop of Rochester, for 15 years, until 2009. He is originally from Pakistan and was the first non-white Diocesan Bishop in the Church of England. He was appointed in 1994. Before that he was the General Secretary of CMS from 1989 to 1994 and prior to holding this position was Bishop of Raiwind in Pakistan. He holds both British and Pakistani citizenship and from 1999 was a member of the House of Lords where he was active in a number of areas of national and international concern. He has both a Christian and a Muslim family background and is now President of the Oxford Centre for Training, Research, Advocacy and Dialogue (OXTRAD).

In this interview, Bishop Michael addresses the State of Western Civilization; it's strengths; what's working really well; the challenges we face. He describes his positive vision for the future-his version of heaven on earth. He believes that we need a spiritual foundation for life and that we are living on past spiritual capital and that Christianity is essential to start regenerating that spiritual capital.

Bishop Michael says what he thinks of being spiritual but not religious-whether or not that is an evolutionary step towards a global post-Ethnic pure form of spirituality without cultural and historical baggage. Could it be that the C of E is the first post postmodern religion which provides a lead for the others in recognizing their common path and accommodating all-the first post-postmodern, Integral, Global religion? He sets out his conditions for that to be possible.

He says we need a shared story of who we are, what we believe, our values and history. He tells his version of that story and his own identity. He celebrates the strengths of Britain and talks about how he personally views the history of the British Empire and how we relate to that today. Clearly he sees Christianity as absolutely the central pillar of our history, identity, culture and values.

Bishop Michael comments upon the muted Western reaction to the persecution of Christians around the world. Why do the Western Elites turn a blind eye?

How do we defend our freedoms, democracy and way of life from those who want to force their authoritarian and absolutist way upon us at a time when the pseudo-liberal elite have made it at least taboo if not illegal to engage in debate and assert that Western or British values are better and in any case are our own right in our own country? What's needed to sort out gang violence and social decay? How do we restore the healthy authority of a parent, teacher, policeman, doctor etc?

Bishop Michael really understands the state we are in the Civilizational challenges we face and has the courage to speak the truth in the face of strong social pressure to stick to the Politically Correct hymn sheet. Visit: http://michaelnazirali.com

**Nicholas:** Bishop Michael, welcome to the series *exploring the Future of Western Civilization.*

**Bishop:** Thank you.

**Nicholas:** Thank you very much for taking part.

**Bishop:** It looks like a very interesting series.

**Nicholas:** For anyone that doesn't know Bishop Michael he originally came from Pakistan and moved to England. He has a both Christian and Muslim family background and he became 106th Bishop of Rochester, a position which he held for 15 years. Prior to that, he was a Bishop in Pakistan in Raiwind Province and in 1999, he was elevated to the House of Lords. He is now President of the Oxford Centre for Training, Research, Advocacy and Dialogue and he has a hugely prestigious academic career across far too many grand institutions to mention but if I mention a few of the titles of his books that will give a flavor. *Conviction and*

*Conflict, Islam, Christianity in the World Order, Unique and Universal Christ: Jesus in a Plural World, Understanding my Muslim Neighbor, The Shape of the Church to Come, Citizens and Exiles: Christian Faith in a Plural Society, Mission in Dialogue, Proclaiming the Gospel Afresh in Every Age* and *Frontiers in a Muslim Encounter.*

The reason personally that I was interested to meet with you Bishop was I've really been impressed that you appear to be, in my view, one of the few leaders in the Church of England who will stand up courageously and boldly speak what I consider to be common sense outside of the politically correct socially acceptable bubble. You've shown immense courage in doing that.

**Bishop:** That's the strange thing about common sense, isn't it, that it's not so common and we wish that it were, of course.

**Nicholas:** Can I start with the very biggest question? Well, actually perhaps not quite. Speaking to a Bishop it's not the biggest question but what is the state of Western Civilization?

**Bishop:** I think in some ways we have to note what is encouraging so respect for the human person, at least in some ways. I can tell you why there is not so much respect as well but on the whole, there is respect for human freedom, for the human person. There is a concern for those who are less able or less privileged than ourselves, a concern for the poor, a concern for victims of natural dictator or a disease. These are all good things about Western Civilization today. Not so much now but in the recent past there has been innovation, creativity, entrepreneurial flair and all of those things than the rest of the world has learned a great deal from the West.

**Nicholas:** Bishop, what do you think are the challenges facing Western Civilization?

**Bishop:** I think there are a number of very important questions that have arisen because of pressure built from within and from without and both need to be kept in mind. I think from within, because the West, at least Europe, has abandoned its foundational principles, which lie, really in the Judeo-Christian tradition and the Bible because it's abandoned many of the beliefs and values that came from that tradition. There are some threats. For instance, whilst there is respect for the human person in one way on the other hand the earliest forms of being a human person are in jeopardy.

**Nicholas:** What do you mean earliest forms?

**Bishop:** I mean we have had (in the UK) 200,000 abortions this year and that's been so since the passing of the Abortion Act, which was actually meant to, you will appreciate this is a doctor, meant to relieve severe hardship but has now become kind of abortion on demand. Then and not surprisingly there is now pressure at the end of the human lifecycle with the growing pressure for assisted suicide and euthanasia. There's the pressure, not just pressure but actually the end of the family is not too strong a way of putting it which is at the root of so many of our problems in society at the moment. Hedonism, self-indulgence without any without any restriction. No society in the past anyway has survived these sorts of pressures because they are pretty fundamental.

From outside …

**Nicholas:** Are you sure about that? Things are they go in cycles, generational cycles. For example, in some of the Victorian period, they would have had a similar periods of drunkenness, and loose sexual morals and so on, and then in the late Victorian era there was an enlightenment phase and a new religious revival. Doesn't it go like that?

**Bishop:** I think we would be very complacent if we thought that. Of course, there are periods of moral and religious spiritual seriousness and periods when a society may not be so serious about these things. Take the example that you've given throughout the Victorian period the basic assumptions of society were stable. That's not to say I agree with all of them and that's not to say that they were uniformly spread throughout society. I think what we've got now is something more radical, which is a questioning and a rejection of foundational principles and I think that is wrong without putting anything in their place. The net result is a kind of vacuum, which is spiritual and moral, and which is dangerous for society.

**Nicholas:** We have had a period in which the old traditional structures were changed, and broken down, deconstructed, relativized, consumerized away and so on. You can look at upon that as a period of vandalism and destruction with negative consequences but another lens through which some people see that it is a necessary evolutionary step where by loosening of the chains of the old way of doing things, we step up into a new way of being. They would say, from a spiritual dimension, the fracturing of the old traditional religious structures is actually an opportunity for us to step forward into the global post-religious, spiritual but not religious dimension where all the different world religions can evolve towards a common deeper truth.

**Bishop:** I think there are lots of things there. The first is that it is the Judeo-Christian tradition that has given the West the basis for self-criticism. The Bible is full of self-criticism. Sacrifice is criticized by the prophets. Kings are criticized, priests are criticized. Jesus was very strong about misuse of the spiritual for commercial and other ends and for hypocrisy and things like that. This very valuable tradition of self-criticism has itself come from the Judeo-Christian tradition from the Bible and we need to acknowledge that. Not every tradition has it. Not every system has it. Totalitarian systems for instance in North Korea. We should not be easily optimistic in transposing evolutionary ideas to social problems. That was exploded, that kind of facile optimism by the First World War and liberal Protestantism, which of course used these ideas, which were found to rather hollow.

I'm quite wary of people who talk easily about evolution in this social sense. I mean the brave worlds to which it leads are often not worlds I particularly want to be in.

**Nicholas:** How about we frame it as a practical question? One of the things you've given a lot of consideration to is how Christianity works in pluralistic society, obviously, in Britain and other Western countries who've had a very high level of immigration including many people of other faiths. Also internally we've had a cultural revolution really and so there are those who are spiritual but not religious or atheists, and so on. How can Christianity be an authority and provide leadership in such a complex society?

**Bishop:** Any authority that Christianity claims must be the authority of service. This is where Christianity is quite different from, say, Islam because Islam in whatever form and for whatever reason believes that you can change the world by taking power. From the cross, Christianity has always believed that you change the world by giving up power. Any authority must be that of service and virtues like service, sacrifice, selflessness are intrinsic. We have got it in society from the Christian tradition. It's not universally available.

I think that's the first thing but on the question of how to cope with diversity, even super-diversity as people now call it. I think the best way in this country anyway would have been to welcome this diversity on the basis of Christian hospitality rather than sort of empty notions of tolerance and leaving things alone, letting people get on with their own lives. We know the result of all that has been segregation, lack of integration and lack of any sense of a common citizenship, things like that. Given Britain's heritage, the right point of departure would have been Christian hospitality, welcoming people and giving ...

**Nicholas:** Does that mean you are welcome as a guest so long as you obey the rules or you can be a member so long you respect the structures?

**Bishop:** I think there has to be first of all a recognition that Britain is where it is because it's come from somewhere. I mean the big mistake about multiculturalism was a kind of amnesia about all of that.

Secondly, for people who come here, of course, to be aware of their own history but particularly in how that helps them to live here and this is not just being aware of your history in vacuum but how it affects them living here.

Thirdly, I think hospitality means welcoming people's contribution to national life, once all of these other things have been recognized.

**Nicholas:** I read that you said that we needed a common shared story of who we are, something for us all to align around and obviously, something that children could be taught. How do you tell that story of who we are?

**Bishop:** You can begin where you like but let's begin in the 6th century with the arrival of Augustine on the mud flats of Kent, and his missionaries having planted a church in Canterbury, and then came to Rochester. Before that what you have is a multiplicity of petty kingdoms, chiefdoms all mutually antagonistic to one another, incessant war and invasion, very little material Civilization, almost no education, etc. The principle for organizing society came from the Christian church. I mean it is still reflected in things like the word "marriage" for instance. The initiative for education came from the church. Theodore of Tarsus, Archbishop of Canterbury and Hadrian the African who came with an established education system in this country for the very first time. Then you have pious Kings like Edward the Confessor and Edmond who established the rule of law, Alfred of course, Alfred the Great. Magna Carta, the reformation, the principle of universal franchise first articulated by Christians in the 17th century.

However, you tell the story; the campaign to abolish the slave trade and later slavery, the arrival of important institutions like nursing, you can't tell the story without talking about the Christian faith. It is impossible and the reason that history is now so uninteresting, a sort of mishmash of names and dates as Michael Gove has pointed out is because the animating principle in the story has been removed.

**Nicholas:** That being the Christian story.

**Bishop:** Yes.

**Nicholas:** The traditional British story was that the British people are the most successful tribe in the world, invented everything, globalized the world, the biggest and best Empire and so on, and all the things that went with that. When that story collapsed because the Empire ended but also the values from which had been founded radically changed, I think, psychologically people have got several options as to how you deal with that. You either live in nostalgia and pretend it hasn't happened. Or you angrily, and in a reactionary conservative way say, let's turn back the clock. Or you go into consumerism or just drugs and pop music, and don't even think about it. Or you push it down into shadow, and stay unconscious, and say, all of that was bad, very bad it was awful, nothing to do with me, and go into the anti-world, which we've been in for a while.

You come from an ex-British colony and you've made the transition over here and straddled both cultures in a complex way. How do you personally tell the story of being someone, a non-white person from Pakistan coming here and integrating? How do you deal with the Empire thing, the racism, and all of that in your story?

**Bishop:** The Empire thing, India was never a colony by the way, it was an Empire. I mean Victoria was Empress of India as much as Queen of England. The imperial story if you like is a very mixed bag. I think you have to acknowledge that. In India, for instance there was a lot of greed associated with what the East India Company did. There was, what's the word, patronizing superiority in terms of for instance, the education system, Macauley saying, "Give me two shelves of English literature and you can all of the books of the Orient that you want." That's a kind of ignorance.

On the other hand, there were many, many achievements. Modern India and Pakistan, modern South Asia would be unrecognizable without the Empire. The civil service, the armed forces, the rule of law, the use of common law in judicial decisions, the railways. Whether you look at material Civilization or cultural intellectuals there's a huge impact that British made.

**Nicholas:** Plus democracy all, though that came afterwards.

**Bishop:** Of course, yes, democracy was begun by the British. There were legislative assemblies and towards the end after the Home Rule Act of 1935, I mean India was a kind of functioning democracy, yes and all of that, of course, with vigorous, vigorous Indian participation. Gandhi would not have survived if he had been battling another more principle-less kind of Civilization. Even the judges that were sending him to jail were apologetic about this. I think all that has to be taken into consideration.

The Empire to some extent did not end but transmuted into a Commonwealth. I think that was a great achievement but not enough was made of it. I think there was a desire because of the Second World War to relate more closely to Europe, to prevent another World War arising from Europe anyway. I think that was to some extent justified but I feel like the Queen on this matter that there is a great deal of value left in the Commonwealth.

**Nicholas:** Could I ask you personally, how do you identify as British, or Pakistani or what?

**Bishop:** Both really. I also think of myself very much as a citizen of the world because I have worked in so many parts of the world but British in the sense that Britain gave me refuge when my life was in danger and that of my family. That itself I think is a value that could easily be lost. Again, stemming from Christian hospitality, the clear teaching of the Bible that we often hear that we are to love our neighbors as ourselves but the Bible teaches we are to love the stranger. Now that tradition of loving the stranger is under threat both from a kind of right wing fascism. Europe may have defeated fascism but it hasn't killed it and from radical Islamism for example, which has its own agenda and therefore threatens the openness of British society.

**Nicholas:** What's your advice from your experience of how we retain our values as being open, and democratic, tolerant, pluralistic, sensitive to others and so on when we have some people with authoritarian views who wish to impose those upon us?

**Bishop:** There must be freedom of speech of course, because that is fundamental and freedom to practice any faith that people wish to practice or not to have a faith at all. Those are fundamental freedoms. I fight for them in other parts of the world. I can't say that they are not necessary here. However, take immigration as an example. Any country must take the needs of the people who are here already into account. Their interests, their jobs, their security, their housing, whatever it maybe. You know, that is the responsibility of any government.

There is then the question of welcoming people who are fleeing persecution, intolerance, whatever it maybe and Britain has a good record of doing that and that's why so many people want to come here.

Thirdly, in the world in which we live, the global situation, every country will need immigration of one kind or another because no country will have all the skills that are needed for this global world. We find increasingly that people overseas own many of our industries, much of our infrastructure and communication systems, and all of that has to be looked after. There will be movement, more free movement of people. However, those who want to come here and to citizens of this country must be familiar with how the country has got here, with the lingua franca, with some view of a common citizenship and ...

**Nicholas:** The main obstacle to that is not the people that come here but I white liberals or pseudo-liberals. People who have a kind of self-hatred and their relativism and their self-loathing that comes with past racism, slavery, and Empire and so on and they feel any assertion of truth, whether it be the Christian authority or whether it be a national identity or whatever, they think it's the next step to Auschwitz and therefore they say, "No, we can't assert anything and people should be free to do whatever they like."

**Bishop:** I mean we've got to find a way in between. The next step to Auschwitz is one kind of fear but what about anarchy? A more real fear is anarchy where there are no fundamental beliefs and values to guide society, to strengthen the family, to give people a reason for living, to be a basis for a plural society and so on. I think that's a very real danger, whilst being aware of the temptations of fascism. We've had a fairly recent manifestation of a most terrible kind of fascism in Europe and we can't forget that obviously, nevertheless we can't slide into anarchy either.

Take racism, the constructive criticism of racism was brought about by bringing the Judeo-Christian tradition to bear on it. Take Slavery. Lecky described England's crusade against slavery as "among the three or four perfectly virtuous acts recorded in the history of nations" How else would that have come about? Where would have the spiritual resources have come from?

Even criticism of what was bad in the Empire and the basis for giving people their freedom. Throughout the Mau Mau situation in Kenya it was Christian leaders, most of them from Britain who were criticizing what was happening.

**Nicholas:** If you look around the world, there's a lot of persecution of Christians going on, very much so in Egypt and some of the other Arab countries. In your own country of origin, in Pakistan, Christians are routinely persecuted and you can argue there's jihad going on in Nigeria, in Kenya, and many other places. Why is it that the West and in particular, as in particular the Church of England is silent on that, with the occasional word but when it's routine that Christians are persecuted no one seems to care. Why is that?

**Bishop:** I think there is actually a greater perception now of what is happening, greater than there has ever has been. David Cameron in speeches in Indonesia for instance was quite revealing. He explicitly pointed to the situations of Christians in the Middle East. I think that has to be welcomed. Sometimes other considerations get in the way. I've been an admirer for a long time of the United States and it's State Department because they have a permanent commission on religious freedom. Each year they issue a report which details all the violations of religious freedom in our world including the ones that you are talking about. It's not just Christian.

I'm very concerned about the situation of the Bahá in Iran, about the Abadia in Pakistan and so on, as a Christian, one must be. But in this splendid collection of violations of religious freedom throughout the world, we then come to Saudi Arabia, and there's a single line which says, "The President has exercised his waiver regarding this country," and there is no information, so what's the reason? Sometimes there is silence.

**Nicholas:** Yes, that's a very good argument for a lot of investment in alternative renewable energy so we free ourselves, so we have energy security and are not dependent on others for that.

**Bishop:** Yes but so much fuss is being made about Iran. It's a country I know well. At many different levels in Iran there are issues causing concern, correctly. However, why should there be this concern about Iran and not a country like Saudi Arabia?

**Nicholas:** Very well said. Bishop Michael when we first met about seven years ago or so, you told me that you felt that Britain was living on, or the West as a whole actually, was living past spiritual capital. Could you say a bit about what that means and also what do we need to do to start renewing our spiritual capital and getting it flowing and the stocks building?

**Bishop:** What I meant was, take a fundamental value like inalienable human dignity to which we all subscribe, it's in the UN Declaration, it's in the European Convention, it's now incorporated into domestic law but does inalienable human dignity actually mean? From where do human beings get this dignity, which cannot be taken away from them? It comes from the Bible's view that human beings are made in God's image. They are not automata; they are not even merely animals. There is something unique about humans, which gives them that dignity which other people cannot take away from them except in tightly prescribed circumstances like self-defense.

You can live on the past capital of believing in inalienable human dignity for a while but sooner or later, it'll come under attack. As I was saying earlier, it has already come under attack at the earliest stages of life and the latest things like metal capacity and when there is a loss of mental capacity those sorts of questions will put this under increasing pressure unless there is a spiritual, religious, metaphysical, however you want to put it, basis of this belief.

Take equality. Why do we believe human beings are equal? On the face of it, they are not. They are differently mentally and physically endowed. They are wealthy and poor. They are black, brown, yellow and white, male and female, thin, fat, tall, short. They are not equal. The one thing if you look at human beings out in the street that is they are not equal. Why do we believe that they are equal? We've got a tremendous equality industry in this country. The answer of course is the Bible's teaching about common origin. That human beings have a common origin in the creation stories. That's why they are equal.

**Nicholas:** Professor Putnam, author of Bowling Alone etc, he wrote a new book called *American Grace*. He looked across the changes in spiritual and religious belief in America and found very much a similar, well on the East and West coast, found a similar pattern to Europe where Christianity has been very much in decline. Obviously, not in the Midwest but that doesn't mean there's …

**Bishop:** Or South, Midwest …

**Nicholas:** Or the South but actually there's been a huge increase in a new group who identify as spiritual but not religious and people from that group, some would be New Age or some would tantric or whatever. That they would say actually what you are talking about you can know that through direct experience, through directly experiencing the divine, or directly experiencing God or the truth, or being and you can feel your own being and the being of the other. We don't need a traditional, it's not that Christianity is wrong but it's just one way of telling the story. Do we really need to tell it the Christian way or?

**Bishop:** What other way are you going to tell it? You can tell it the Dalai Lama's way. He's hugely popular among these people you are talking about. That means the Dalai Lama's story means there's no transcendent being, there is no self and those who hold to a transcendent being or to the reality of the self are deceived, self-deceived perhaps. How can you be self-deceived if there's no self? I think we must appreciate the radicalness of what looks attractive on the outside. The Dalai Lama has just been given the Templeton Prize for religion. Fine, but it's not the same religion as Christianity.

Secondly, of course, it is true that all human beings have an innate sense I believe of the spiritual dimension of life. I think this is correct but religion is not just that. Religion is the social expression of the spiritual and it you abandon that social expression of the spiritual you open yourself in the end to moral anarchy. The reason that Western intellectuals are willing to talk about the spiritual but not the religious is because of this over individualistic, hedonistic, consumeristic culture into which we are caught.

**Nicholas:** Right, so there's no discipline holding one's ego in check.

**Bishop:** Yes, it's not just that. It's things like what is the basis for law, for instance? What is the basis for values? Wider than law? Things like that, which only religion can provide and which why it is so unpopular.

**Nicholas:** Bishop, can I ask you? What is your vision of Heaven on Earth? If all of your beliefs and values came true, were made real, what would be that be like?

**Bishop:** Reinhold Niebuhr said that democracy is possible because of the goodness of human beings. It is necessary because of their wickedness. I am not looking for a perfect society. I don't think there ever will be a perfect society. Human beings are a mixture of good and bad. The aim should be to maximize the common good and to minimize what is bad in society. Given that I think, a democracy is, as they say, the worst of all systems except for all of the rest. It's the best of a bad job but with the Arab spring, particularly I have come to see that democracy needs to be hedged around with other things. A Bill of Rights for instance that guarantees fundamental freedoms. Some affirmation of one law for all. The equality of all before the law. Common citizenship if we are to avoid, in the Islamic context, a return to the Dhimmi where non-Muslims are second class citizens, where women are second class and so on.

I look for a democratic society, which nevertheless has checks, and balances, which doesn't work by opinion poll and focus groups but has fundamental beliefs and values which can themselves be criticized of course, but that's not a reason for a complete abstinence.

Heaven on Earth I believe, of course, God is working His purposes out in this world. We can be collaborators with God in the building of society but I also believe in the transformation that the Gospel brings into people's lives and how that affects society. There is now a very interesting discipline in sociology looking at how Christianity in particular is changing societies in Latin America, in India, in Africa and so on. Quite a lot of hard data about that.

**Nicholas:** I saw it. I don't know if you saw it the other day there was a BBC series about the church and it ended a way that surprised me that the chap who was telling the story. He went through the history of the way the Church of England, because it is the established church, has to adapt to newcomers and not just in the last 50 years. He ran all the way through the different groups who've come here and also just the natural pluralism within the country telling lots of interesting stories about how the church accommodated them. He brought it right up to date in Leicester which is one of the most ethnically and religiously diverse places and he showed an example of where the Church of England using the cathedral to bring in people of all types, of different faiths, and also of different versions of Christianity and the full spectrum of atheists, agnostic. His point was that the future evolution of the Church of England is to actually be the first, this is my language, the first post-postmodern integral church that can actually get a structure that honors, the truth and all of the different paths and brings them together, the most mature religion, the most advanced, getting to a global level. Does that make sense to you or is that just wishy-washy relativism?

**Bishop:** What any Christian church must do is to engage with people where they are and to take full account of their experience, and of truth, goodness perhaps more importantly that there is already. That has then to be related to the Christian story. If a church abandons that then it doesn't remain a Christian church any more. As I was saying, there are stories that are radically different from the Christian story. Buddhism is a very fine model and spiritual system but it is based on views that are completely contrary to Christian ideas about, for example, the human person. Hinduism again, is a very fine religious and moral system or series of systems but many of the things that Hinduism believes in quite different from the Judeo-Christian worldview.

This is not to say there's nothing of value. We need to learn from other views, and other systems, and other religions but having a clear vantage point of our own. This has been the difficulty in postmodernism is that people are not given any vantage point of their own. Schoolchildren are taught in religious education a kind of smorgasbord of all sorts of exotic religious practices but they are not told from what point of view they are to assess, and evaluate and accommodate to these different beliefs and practices.

**Nicholas:** My family came from the inner city and although I grew up in the suburbs, my grandparents were still in the inner city on Council Estates. They were subject frequently to violence and crime, and racism, and gang activity. Their sense was that the world was falling apart. The police couldn't do anything. The parents were not disciplining their children. The fabric was falling apart. My observation is that the church is not very good at being assertive, of saying, "No, that's wrong. Stop it. Get out. That's bad." It's like in the balance of masculine and feminine it's been emasculated and feminized. I don't know if it's the First World War that did that or past abuses or whatever. Islam is very strong on clear boundaries and authority. What's your position on that? When someone is living in an inner city area with decay, social decay, how can you restore that to righteousness and security?

**Bishop:** There are many reasons why we are in this situation but the most basic has been the dissolution of the family because people learn basic beliefs, values in the family. Where that is concerned even more the disappearance of the father. Parents are not as it were interchangeable with one another. How a father relates to children is quite different from how a mother relates to children. In their nurture children need both. We've tried to shove the responsibility of the family onto the school. The school is not able to do what families can do and even then, we've taken away nearly every sanction of discipline.

**Nicholas:** How can a teacher or a parent have authority if they don't believe in anything?

**Bishop:** The refusal to believe. I think assemblies are such vacuous affairs in schools because teachers because teachers have been brought up not believing in anything. I don't think myself that a lot of this is simply accidental. Some of it maybe, as you were saying, a reaction to the past but that has actively been used by political and social constructivists. If you consider people like Marcuse, Gramsci and neo-Marxism, this activist theory of revolution that you must undermine the bourgeoisie structures of society I think they did influence some professions, some of the unions in some of the things that we saw in 60s, 70s, 80s, even.

Then I think in the Anglo-Saxon context we also have people who borrowed the criticism of social institutions from the neo-Marxists but instead of them being a prelude to political revolution they became ends in themselves and the reconstruction or the deconstruction of the families is one of the most prominent in this.

**Nicholas:** Do you mean they deliberately undermined it as a tactic to bring in a new form of power?

**Bishop:** A new form of freedom I think they would say. They see...

**Nicholas:** They see them as abusive old structures.

**Bishop:** Yes, Harold Pinter, I don't know if you saw his film called *The Family?* It was just trying to show how dysfunctional and oppressive it was and of course, that's true. That's true of anything human that it can become like that. R D. Laing, psychiatry again had a full quest on the oppression of the family. I don't think the family has been under this kind of sustained attack in any Civilization before.

**Nicholas:** Finally, when you're dealing with people like that, with those beliefs can you argue with them, persuade them to your point of view or is that waste of breath?

**Bishop:** I think there is just criticism of where human institutions go wrong whether that is in politics, or religion or family but to say on the basis of that there must be no such institution is the fallacy. That is the fallacy into which many of us have fallen and I wouldn't agree with that. The evidence is there for all to see. All the research tells us that the best outcome is from children who are in a stable family. All the research is showing fathers make a difference. This is not just a dogmatic assertion. It's backed up by reasonable research.

**Nicholas:** Okay. Finally thank you very much Bishop Michael for a fascinating interview.

**Bishop:** Thank you.

**Nicholas:** If anyone would like to get in touch with you or follow your past or present work, what web address would you recommend?

**Bishop:** Well under my own name at http://michaelnazirali.com.

**Nicholas:** Great. Thank you very much.

# German Identity & Patriotism

## Healing the Wounds, Integrating the Shadow

**Adrian Wagner interviewed by Dr Nicholas Beecroft**
Adrian is an emerging German leader. Aged 26, from the Millennial Generation "X," he writes on social transformation and integral consciousness. In this interview, he discusses German Identity and Patriotism; the state of German consciousness, it's healing and integration. He sets out his highest vision for Germany, the West and Global civilization.

He begins with his personal journey from what he calls a "liberal-left" to an integral consciousness. He describes his experience of processing the shadow cast by the Nazi period and coming to a more healthy, integrated and positive modern German identity and patriotism. Adrian believes that we need a positive, healthy national consciousness alongside our global, personal and other identities.

We discuss what constitutes the boundary between a positive patriotism and a darker nationalism and racism. He brilliantly describes the role of healthy boundaries, self-confidence and assertiveness from the individual level to the national level. We test out how this applies to multiculturalism and in particular the integration of the Turkish Diaspora into Germany. Does he agree with Chancellor Merkel said that "Multikulti" had failed?

What's a better, more positive vision for the future? Adrian gives his view on how Germany can assume its leadership role in Europe, particularly in the context of the Euro crisis. He finishes with his perspective on the British-German relationship.

Adrian Wagner is someone to watch. Whatever path he follows, it'll be something very interesting and transformational. At age 28, he is already writing on cultural transformation, values and integral world views. He trained in Spiral Dynamics with Don Beck, Theory U with Otto Scharmer,

Tai Chi practice in India and at the end of his degree in Social Work. He participated in Field studies in value systems in the Middle East, India and the Philippines. Currently Adrian is developing with friends the YouthLeaders Program in the "Karma Youth" Project in Germany. He is studying Voice Dialogue with Cordula Mears-Frei and working as a freelancer for several Magazines related to Social Threefolding, integral Theory and Anthroposophy in a postmodern context.

**Nicholas:** Adrian Wagner, welcome to the series exploring the Future of Western Civilization.

**Adrian:** Thanks, Nicholas, for inviting me. I'm very much looking forward to have this conversation about German identity here right now.

**Nicholas:** Excellent. As Adrian says, the focus is about German identity and how that is evolving. Also, we're going to start off talking a bit about Adrian's own personal journey through his, I suppose, from a liberal-left type of consciousness to an integral consciousness.

By way of introduction, Adrian is German. He was born in Ludwigsburg near Stuttgart. He's 28 years old placing him as a Generation Y, Millennial. He already is a writer on social transformation and integral thinking. He's right at the end now of a Social Work Degree. Although, you'll know after a few minutes of him speaking, he's not the average social worker and, if he does do that, he'll be transforming it. He's definitely an emergent German leader.

He is trained in Spiral Dynamics, Tai Chi, Theory U. He has a fascinating story to tell about his own experience living those theories in the Middle East and India. Currently, he's training in a brilliant process called Voice Dialogue, which I highly recommend. I'll let you tell him the last bit himself. He's with a group called Development Lab a Generation Next project. Could you say a bit about that Adrian?

**Adrian:** Generation Next for me is just like a word to describe the people that are my age and that I engage with integral theory or those new kind of ideas. It's not actually a group per se, but it's something like how I would describe our generation. It's the generation that will make the next step. It's the Generation Y.

We are moving to make the next step forward. I find that quite terrific and it just fits. Friends, a lot of my friends feel the same way. Specifically in Germany where I'm working now. We have a group. The group is called DevelopmentLab. We work with each other and belong to this kind of broader wave, global wave that I would call "Generation Next."

**Nicholas:** Great. Now, the core topic is German identity and German patriotism, German consciousness. We've got two blonde-haired, blue-eyed men talking about that subject and, me, with a German flag behind me. Obviously, we have to be mindful that the average politically correct person will probably be absolutely horrified by that. Therefore, we need to establish that this isn't part of some Neo-Nazi youth movement or something.

What better subject to bring up than to hear of your journey, your own conscious journey from being, as you'd described it to me, being a liberal-left type person to an integral person? Could you briefly talk us through that? How did you change your mindset? How did it grow?

**Adrian:** I'm glad that we started at that place. For me, it begins really around age 17, the first time I discovered Yoga and I started to practice Yoga and I started to read certain books like Paolo Coelho. I got into youth trainings. At that time, I really was searching for meaning.

I was also a wrestler at that time and at a business school. I came really to this place where I just had a big crisis. I thought, "Wow! What to do with my life?" I felt, "Whoa! Children and nature," that was the next step that came up out of nothing. That business perspective, all numbers and money, I felt like, "That's mean."

I moved and I went into an environmental year. That's something like the civil service just in the environment. I became very happy in that year because a had a lot of things to do and I really could work out of myself and out of self-interest in protecting nature, saving nature, and organizing trainings but also organizing a festival together with other young people. It's also a pretty nice system. It really made me understand how democracy functions in Germany with a delegate system where you move to meetings on a broader level in Germany.

All of that led me to a youth and culture center in Stuttgart because I really had more of a spiritual yearning connected to the Yoga practice and also I am connected a bit to my Christian roots but I just could not combine it and I really had a hard time with that. I also couldn't deal with Buddhism. That was too much nothingness for me at that time.

I would describe myself at that time very liberal, very romantic, and very green. I moved into a cultural youth center that was then in Stuttgart. There, I started a year to work in a sector where they give seminars and lectures. It's not just a usual seminar center. It's a center that has grown out of the '68 movement but has a specific and a philosophic background in a liberal fashion mixed with anthroposophy.

A lot of what was coming at me in that time, in that year, was there was so many different perspectives and they have also the specific focus in that year in the seminars and lecture series like Israel-Palestine and also the German past. I was introduced at a very young age of 18 into a very big topic and it was, for me, the first time to really be emotionally confronted with that painful experience. I recall this experience where I was sitting in a lecture and I just needed to leave it. It was the first time I really felt we lost something in Germany. We really lost something. That was the beginning of a journey towards my German identity.

That was really working within me. At the same time, it was very pluralistic. We had also workshops on the Wall, workshops on the struggle of the Palestinians. We had workshops from the Israeli men who helped to found a Kibbutzim in a more holistic fashion.

There were so many perspectives in that time, some wise and some not so wise. It just really brought me into a state of confusion. In a way, I was praying, "Give me something where I can handle all of this information and all of those perspectives. Give me something. I want to understand. I want to know. I want to see the bigger picture."

I really felt lost and it was not so much mentally. It was much more physically. There's a sense that something is not quite fitting. Something is not quite right but nobody gives you this tool or this kind of perspective who says, "Yes. You put this there and you put this there, you put this there."

**Nicholas:** You mean just overwhelmed by complexity-so many different world views that it blew your mind to hold them all at once.

**Adrian:** Yes. Definitely. It was a very fascinating experience as well. It was a reflection of myself. To see that there are certain world views that are just really highly moral but, at the same time, you also get certain world views, certain energies that are just really not so ... they don't feel moral, not so high developed on a feeling level.

There was a lot of conflict going on as well in the center and in myself as well at that time. I really wanted to understand what is going on in Israel, Palestine. That was a strong focus. Right at the end, I discovered in a paper (Info3) that I'm writing now for as a freelancer, they had a big series about Ken Wilber. I just saw his picture on the front and opened it. I found these four quadrants to which he often refers and it really worked for me, too.

I just was, "That's it." I really got into reading Wilber and just got stuck into reading the books. They're like, "Wow! Okay." This is the model I was trying to find. This is what I was searching for to have this bigger 50,000 feet view. I just finished the first book and wanted to keep reading but then I was already on my track to Israel-Palestine which was quite an adventure.

I landed there also with a group from Europe who did something like a peace training. I felt, "Yes. Let's see how they do." You just go with them and it was pretty crazy. We walked from the Sea of Galilee to Jerusalem. We had a lot of experience. I saw a lot of people. We went into the territories of West Bank. We had Israelis with us who are actually not allowed to go there so it was quite a group process.

I stayed afterwards for almost five months in the region but, at that time, I really felt that Europeans come and they have a vision. They want peace and then they leave after three weeks. It just didn't feel 100% right. Specifically, the group had a strong moral sense of what should be done, they wanted to build peace villages. You need to stop war. It felt very naïve in a way. It didn't even feel that it was very much grounded in reality. For me ...

**Nicholas:** They go away feeling very good about themselves.

**Adrian:** Exactly. On a certain level, it's very much connected to your own history, to your own identity, to your own sense of belongingness. There is a lot of projection going on. That was also very interesting for me to see and to feel on a personal level to discover how much I projected on the Israelis and Palestinians.

**Nicholas:** Germany went through the most massive experiences in the Twentieth Century. When were you born? You were two when Germany reunified. As a young person in Germany, what's your experience of that legacy?

**Nicholas:** In a way, it depends on where you want to start it. The war is definitely is still also in my generation very vivid. My grandfather was in prison in Russia. He even talked Russian. The war was there. In a way I was very free. I had a very abundant youth. It was really amazing to grow up in the '90s. There was so much richness and so much energy still available. For Germany, in particular, I would say that one of the real difficulties that came with the war was to neglect yourself in a certain sense like your identity and to just keep going.

After the war, people just went on and they built Germany up in 50 years. It was destroyed and look how it looks now. It was such incredible work they have done but a lot of the work was done in the outside. You even had a psychological syndrome. My teacher at the university told me that, once, people, they really would work until they totally finished. Today, you would call it burnout but it was something similar but a bit different.

They couldn't process the traumatic experience of the war so they would just keep working. I guess they had to, it was a sort of coping mechanism. They would just keep working. To a certain degree, it was, I understand, it was necessary but, in another level, this emotional work wasn't fully done.

I also think, my generation is the first generation that is a bit more objective. You can take a look more from the outside because you were not involved in the war. Then, your parents, they were not really involved but your grandfather. It's different, there's much more time in which things can come up.

Those things, they're passed on. If you go and deal with it, you carry the same patterns like a lot of guilt, self-esteem issues. When the football team Bayern-Munich lost, the newspapers were asking, "Are we not winners? Do we not want to win?" I feel there's some truth in it to understand or to accept the greatness and the richness of the culture and identity at one level. On another level, how hard is it to really love yourself as a German? There are some difficulties around that definitely.

**Nicholas:** Why? What happens if you feel a healthy patriotism for Germany? It's great to be a German. Germany's a great country albeit with a very dark period in its history but that's a short period in the long perspective of German consciousness.

**Adrian:** I would say that there's nothing wrong with it. It's very great and it also feels very great. It's difficult in the sense that you would have to give up a certain kind of victim position and you would have to take, really take responsibility for the actions and for all the emotions that are still there. You see it from your inner world and that would mean you have a different responsibility for the world as well as for yourself and the world.

**Nicholas:** You said, "would" but you have processed this. Can you say how you've done that yourself? How have you processed that for yourself?

**Speaker 2:** I have processed it and I'm still in this continued process. For me, it means if you bring it down to a personal level, it all comes to relationships, for example. It comes to our relationships to other people and how do you deal with relationships, how do you deal with yourself in relationships. What is your focus? Do you really relate to other people? Are you in contact with other people?

This is something that I think is a quality that is very important for us. Also, can you be kind to yourself? It sounds very liberal but, to a certain extent, it's very necessary and, at the same time, I'm very engaged and very much having conversation on leadership. How do you lead in a healthy way?

For me, I find processes like the Voice Dialogue where you really can look at this different voices and see where is your inner Nazi? Where is this Nazi past in yourself and where is this kind gentle man where there's a true figure that moves forward? Those are all voices in us and it's so important to be aware of them and not to judge them because those energies are still there. It's a choice whether you let yourself be unconsciously led by them or you can become aware of them and choose a different voice to follow.

**Nicholas:** What do you mean there? Does it mean if one has an inner Nazi just like you might have an inner baby or an inner mother, all of our different parts, you're saying you shouldn't judge that?

**Adrian:** Definitely not in the sense that you say, "This doesn't belong to me, this is bad." It's important to say this is a part of a human being and it's pretty easy to get into those traps as we have to be really careful not to allow this part to take hold of ourselves or to guide us. Look, in Germany, there was recently this big wave of Neo-Nazi terrorism going on just half a year ago where people really got woken up.

You can suppress your national identity. I have heard this often from Germans who said, "I'm not German. I'm not German. I'm a global citizen." A healthy sense of a national identity can protect people from becoming radical.

That's why I think it's very important in public when people are moving and coming forward with their nationalistic ideas. You really have to judge it. Definitely, you really have to say, "No. This is not the path. This is not where we need to go."

**Nicholas:** What is the distinction you're making then between a healthy positive patriotism and an unhealthy negative one?

**Adrian:** For me, for example, one very important question is how do you define nationality and do you connect it to something like the cultural realm, all the art, all the music, all that we have produced? In certain sense, more from a creative level. The language, for example, if you view this as culture and as part of a national identity, it has been engaged with different cultures as well but produces a certain pattern in itself which I will call a German identity. If you talk about that, I say that this is quite healthy.

What becomes unhealthy is when people start to really move themselves into the whole race issue. When you say that a German is only somebody that has three generations of German forefathers, then, you connect identity with the biological, a very strong idea that sets borders based upon physical characteristics.

Of course, Germany also has a territory and that's it. It's good to have borders in a certain sense but I'm very much also in favor of coming closer to Europe. If you come back to the protectionist place, for instance, you say, no, we only want to have only Germans here and German identity is defined by race, then, it becomes certainly not healthy.

**Nicholas:** Adrian, ultimately, it depends on your belief system. German, British, these things are meaningless if you look at us as animals or as conscious beings, if you look at the whole history of life across thousands of years. It, currently has some meaning that you mentioned but, really, why not take this as an opportunity just to bin all that old stuff and just go straight for a global consciousness in which we're all just simply human beings and global? Why even bother with a national identity? Why not just say that's badly damaged, let's consign it to the history books?

**Adrian:** That's a great idea and, if it would work, I would say let's just do it. I truly believe we live in a holarchy. We have natural hierarchies and you shift your identity from more egocentric to ethnocentric to world-centric to kosmocentric.

I would say all of those play together and they still need to be in harmony in a certain sense, healthy. What happened in Germany, we had a very strong national identity and it was totally crushed. It was really put into an extreme, into a very ethnocentric place where tribal consciousness in a way hitchhiked even rational thought and technology and you saw what you can do with it. You can build Auschwitz with it. That's definitely not something that we want to have for this world and for humanity. Definitely not. To say let's move just further is something that I think and bypasses the healing of this stage, this very hot topic, which you need to grow through and then you need to keep those different stages well integrated.

**Nicholas:** I will suppose that's where the wounding is because of the past abuse of national or group identity or cultural identity and patriotism. The tendency as you say was to focus on working very hard and being very good economically and of going to the other extreme of being anti-German or getting into the multicultural ideology of celebrating diversity and celebrating the other but hating the self. We've covered that really. Just to be really positive, to forget all of the historical baggage, why right now are you proud to be a German?

**Adrian:** That's a good question. In a certain sense, I'm very proud of what is really moving on and also on an environmental level. That's one of the topics in which that Germany is really pioneering something. We're getting rid of the atomic plants. We still don't know how and I hope there will be a good plan on how to do it. In a sense of what has happened on an environmental level with the Green Party is something that I'm quite proud of. A lot of Germans could relate to that. That's one level.

The other level is that if I look at also the political diversity we have right now in Germany with a totally new party coming up, the Pirates, they've come up, shows me that we don't live like, for example, like the US in a two-party system of which I'm also quite proud. We have a political landscape that is diverse.

And then, there's another level that is more subtle. When I see Berlin, when I visit Berlin, I experience this field that is happening there. There are so many people from abroad coming. There's a whole movement of social entrepreneurship starting funky businesses and all those initiatives. There's really something happening.

There's this sense more and more, again, people who are also my age or people who are really on the forefront that find this connectedness to the country and to a certain philosophical stream which is called idealism but in a different fashion, much more calm, more pragmatic, and not naïve. This is something I really feel is blossoming. The poetry you have in Germany, the art, the music you have too, very long and old tradition.

I just feel at home. It's so important. It's part of my country. Even the earth that you stand on, the ground you stand on, from inside to the outside, a certain softness is breaking through and there's a lot of love. There's a lot of gentleness. I am sensing in Germany that this is reawakened.

**Nicholas:** Love for what?

**Adrian:** Love for life. I would say love for life. We have experienced the shadow but it could also be the opposite I believe. Germany could really be a place where you nurture life and, really, the beauty of life, the German forest, for example, the German connection to nature.

Those are things that I feel very connected to and, in a certain way, also proud. If things are done in Germany, I have the feeling that they really get thought through. Sometimes, we're still a bit too pragmatic. We lack a bit of a broader vision and idealism. We are really down to earth. It's also something I really highly appreciate. This groundedness combined with this new blossoming.

**Nicholas:** You're a visionary guy. What is your vision for a vibrant positive Germany situated within Europe, situated within the world? What's your highest vision for Germany?

**Adrian:** What is my highest vision for Germany? Let's put it that way. For example, imagine Germany would be a place where you really invite all people from different countries, leaders from different sectors and really go through processes where you deal with cultural and national identity and really move forward, projects that serve this global identity. Germany could really be a place to do this. There's a huge integral community starting and moving forward. There are lots of initiatives.

One the visions I have involves an old airport in Berlin, Tempelhof. It's very interesting because it reflects both sides. The Nazis used it but it was also a place where Berlin was held during the time with the Soviets. It was also the place where the American and British airplanes dropped their stuff. Now, Berlin is thinking what to do with this place. Imagine you would have a landing strip for the future.

As Otto Scharmer describes it in Theory U is which also related to the work of Goethe and Goethean Science. His vision or what he brings forward is this "presencing". You sense in the present, what wants to emerge. This is something that Germany can be good at if we allow ourselves.

I don't know if you have heard about Otto Scharmer. He is connecting a lot of German philosophical streams, also in science, using what you call presencing, to sense the present and see what wants to emerge from the future-like building landing strips for the future and to prototype new systems.

I have a strong sense that Germany and the vision of Germany is connected to that because we have such a strong integral community. We have such strong young people that really want to do something. Also, we are pioneers already in the environmental field, more on the exterior. I have a sense here. In my generation, more and more that there's internal work in combination with the external work which is starting to happen, the integration. For that, you would also need people from Europe, from UK, from US to go through this process together.

My personal vision is to imagine youth camps where you have Israeli, Palestinian, English youth, and German youth. If you really go through those national identities, you really work on them and you really develop art out of it like a theater piece or something and you really grow together but not from where do we come from, what is our history, and what's our difference.

**Nicholas:** It's not only Germany that has a wounded or damaged national psyche or national soul. Just about every other country does as well in its own way.

**Adrian:** In a way, I'm also proud of how we have dealt with our past. There's no other country in this world that has, from an analytic perspective, done so much work in understanding or trying to understand how it did happened. This is something we can share with others. We also need to move on.

This is also a global problem, other people and other regimes had it, too. We should not make it too big, not to elevate it into a place where it becomes some mythic or dehumanized ideal.

**Nicholas:** Also, by looking back exclusively, at the Germans or the Nazis, as the almost unique example of evil that actually distracts from the fact that a lot of evil has been done by a lot of different people and actually is still being done. I very much conscious of the risk of that kind of fascism, nationalist absolutism emerging in the Islamic world. Also, in China, there's a very strong risk of nationalism. There's a lot of nationalism in China, a lot of supremacist thinking and so on. By focusing on it in Germany or just on Western people, we miss the risk of future forms of that kind of thing coming up in other countries, in other places-history repeating itself in a different way.

Cultural shadow, in my view, one of the ways in which we've mis- or only semi-processed, our cultural shadow, is that, say, in the German case or going from Nazism, from that kind of absolutistic tribal, racist, supremacist thinking to a healthy form, then going on to pluralistic democracy and going to human rights and so on. Germany has clearly made that transition.

In terms of the national consciousness or the national identity, we have put it into the shadow by going to the multicultural ideology which in its most healthy form is a global perspective seeing many people from many different cultures, great deal of complexity celebrating all of that, being open to all of that in a very positive natural good way.

In it's unhealthy form, the multicultural ideology is being about idealizing the other where the other is naively, falsely celebrated victim group who is elevated as being special and untouchable. And then, there's the in-group which in your case is German or, in my case, British, which is uniquely the receptacle of all badness and must be at best denied if not deconstructed and hated which is really, really badly unhealthy. When your Chancellor, Angela Merkel, said that multiculturalism has failed, what do you think about that?

**Adrian:** True multiculturalism for me, personally, I think really has failed. Multiculturalism is also a concept I'm not so much referring to. I'm much more into transcultural ideas or a transcultural concept where you see that, first of all, national and cultural identities always have been in an exchange.

On one level, it's not easy to also see what is German and what is not German. On the other level, to just live next to each other and to not care-you do what you do, I do what I do. That happened in Germany for a long time. The guest workers-a lot really believed they would go home.

You would have those big parts of your own culture, you would have subcultures in your own cultures and, as long as there was a traditional center still present in Germany, more traditional values, this works pretty well because they could just, they could be next to each other.

Once you move in more into complex thinking and more into pluralistic societies and then the guest workers' children, they grow up and they just have real difficulties with their own identity because they're not German and they're not Turkish, for example. They go to Turkey and they say you're a German and they go to Germany and are called Turks. In a sense, they grow up in a very isolated environment.

There are still certain belief systems that come from the parents, that come from Turkey and that really conflicts with certain German values and certain German identity, stereotypes maybe even. What can you do? Multiculturalism, even the idea that minorities just can do what they want and Germans are the bad guys. That's really not working. That has nothing to do ...

**Nicholas:** Also, it's racist.

**Adrian:** It's racist.

**Nicholas:** Multiculturalism is based on the ideology that there is an us, there are them, and they need to be separate, kept in a separate place, have separate rights and separate identity as opposed to us all being complex individuals.

**Adrian:** That's why I really like the term transcultural because there you see, you can transcend the idea that you're German or that you're just Turkish and that you really have to learn that those difference are there from the upbringing. I'm not neglecting them because that happens often in multiculturalism that you say, "You know, we're all human beings, let's not look at the hot topics."

And then, if you go deeper, most of the time, you're going to find out that those hot topics around maybe marriage or around relationships or around work ethics or whatever, you're going to find out that those topics are often related also to consciousness, to a certain level of understanding the world and to a certain world views.

For example, some of the Turkish population in Germany, they don't want multiculturalism. They want the Christian Democratic Party. You would think why? They're Muslims. Of course, because they represent their values. They're more traditional. They come more from a traditional background. This is something I feel is very important to understand as well.

**Nicholas:** In 2005, when those bombs went off in London they were done by the mostly children of Pakistani descent or one was of Jamaican origin. It was strange because I really felt for them. Obviously, what they did was evil and wrong. That goes without saying. I could really feel that one can understand their alienation because if they grow up in an environment, a very narrow environment where their parents and their parents friends and their local community live like a foreign country within Britain in that case or maybe Turks living in Germany, that itself is outdated. It's not like the modern Pakistan or the modern Turkey. It's the Turkey or Pakistan of 40 years ago.

Around them, they see the negative aspect of Britain or Germany. They see British culture, German culture denigrating itself and saying, "We hate ourselves. We're all racists. Everything about us is bad."

That's not a club you'd really want to join, would you? What can be done to make Germany a more positive club to join, a more attractive open healthy club for young people of Turkish origin within Germany such that they would really love it and want to fit in, become part of it, celebrate it, and make it their own?

**Adrian:** I love that question. First of all, I want to say it's already happening. In a certain sense, this is already happening, of course, maybe also in the academic world. I have a friend. She is of Turkish background and she did her Masters' here in Freiburg in Environmental Studies.

She started a tango project and she really loves to live here. She really enjoys the beauty of Germany. She got a really good education. She had the chance to really move here and to study. For her, I have a sense that life here is really good. She really enjoys it.

This is something that I would like to stress on that topic. First of all, we could profit from people that are educated that bring their cultural richness. We also have to understand what are we good in and what they have to offer. In a certain way, what do we need and what is in for us as well.

The difficulty is that you have grown and it's similar in France or in England, in all those area where you have a lot of immigrants with very poor perspective and vision. The basic thing is, and that relates to social work, give them a vision. Give them a dream. Give them something they can believe in. If you come and say, "Look, the system is bad. Everything is bad. You're just really bad and we hate ourselves." It won't help them. You won't.

You really have to first look, do your own work in a certain sense and then make agreements together with people but also show clear boundaries where you say no. You're not going to cross this. You're not going to cross boundary of human rights. We're not going to let you practice Sharia in our country. Those are our values and, actually, we are quite proud of them.

This is a complex thing. You would have to look into very specific programs and projects for different areas. You cannot just say this is the idea and you're just going to do that. The conversation we are having right now and also being aware of your own identity is already a lot. That could shift something in that direction because what I have experienced is different and what I have read about different Turkish, young people, if they come from a traditional background, honor is very important, something very important in their lives and it can be on a very unhealthiest aspect like they even kill their sisters because she was not honorable for the family.

This is something very, very far off for Germans. Turks will never respect you if you come to them and you try to duck yourself under. This is something we could, for example, in that relationship learn, to really stand our ground.

**Nicholas:** If you are submissive...

**Adrian:** If you're submissive. Exactly. If you're submissive Turks will never respect you. They really need a strong sense of purpose and also a strong kind of leadership and they will love you.

**Nicholas:** When one is dealing with someone from a value system which really values honor and power and, probably its shadow side has shame in it, you said that if you deal with that value system in a submissive, appeasing way, that they would perceive as weakness and disrespect you.

Of course, the fear coming from the German past or the British past would be that to be assertive and to have strong clear boundaries is just step away from fascism or whatever. A lot of the oversensitivity and a lot of the desperate need to be very, very super sensitive is a reaction against the abuses of the past.

How did you get that balance right? How do Germans be assertive in a healthy positive way without tipping over into fascism but in a way that's respectable to people from value systems that respect power and authority?

**Adrian:** That's certainly not an easy question. I can't give you a clear solution-otherwise you would have to be afraid.

**Nicholas:** Have you ever seen it done well?

**Adrian:** Just because you cross boundaries with other people in a very bad way like you did with fascism, it doesn't mean that now you're going to the victim perspective and into shame perspective and don't have any boundaries at all and be a victim. That doesn't work. Unfortunately, that's often what happens psychologically and also, on a collective level, that happened I feel in Germany.

There was a whole generation trained in not having healthy boundaries. It was like an integral abuse on almost all levels. The Nazi regime, they started very young. They did it very professionally, even with the kids. Those are issues where you really can start moving forward and build new systems. Build school systems, for example, where people respect each other's boundaries and where you really learn how, what does it mean to have healthy boundaries on an emotional level, on a physical level, on a spiritual level.

This is something you need to learn and this is something we need to train ourselves in. This is something, from my personal experience, it's a process. It doesn't stop or finish and it's a work that continues to be done. When you meet people like you said, people that have a high respect for honor and for strength. Show them strength, but it's not a strength that comes from the mind or from the perspective or from harshness.

For example, what you have in the Eastern tradition in Aikido or other Martial arts, you take the energy and turn it around. When you are the most vulnerable and the most present, you are often the most strongest. It freaks people out and, of course, a lot of people think, "I just have to be strong and that's it." That's not it. It's vulnerability. Part of it is vulnerability. It is something very different from weakness. To be vulnerable, and at the same time, strong and assertive, it is not a contradiction.

**Nicholas:** That sounds absolutely wonderful. What a leader you are and are going to be with that kind of thinking, that kind of being. Let me parachute you then into the stadium where the Turkish, the football stadium where the Turkish Prime Minister, a couple of years ago, was addressing in the middle of Germany but addressing it almost like, it came across to me like a Nazi rally really, a Hitler-Nuremberg type speech that he gave to young, should be Germans but they're Turks. What do you do about that? That's a massive boundary violation. How do you deal with that in a healthy way that's going to have a happy outcome?

**Adrian:** I know what you're referring to. He was saying, "You are all Turks and you belong to Turkey and, Please vote for me." Basically, for me, it was really like a call for power and to stay in power because he knows if he gets the Turks in Germany, they can vote in Turkey. It was a politically motivated speech. That was my first impression.

The other impression is that you have to understand a lot about Turkey in the way nationalism plays in Turkey. Turkey is only a democracy because it became very nationalist. They have a very strong wound around their religion and spirituality cultural heritage and the national democratic system.

They didn't make the shift into modernity where they could integrate their religion into the cultural realm. That's why you have such a gap there as well. Turkey could be a role model because they already have democracy in a certain way, unlike a lot of Arab countries.

On the other hand, I will agree. It is a certain violation of boundaries on a collective level because young people could, if they don't identify with Germany or if they don't identify with the place they're living, it's very difficult. For me, ideally, we help people to understand that they still can have to a certain degree a Turkish identity and a German identity. That's the work with Voice Dialogue or with other techniques. For sure, it's not something for the masses yet. Definitely not yet. You need at least leaders who are able to carry that message and to have that sense of understanding.

I would say what happened with the speech, if it is built into a process where the ones who are more audible use it in a certain way to help Turkey as well as Germany then we might go along with it until we find better solutions. If it's really only out of nationalistic perspective, then you really have to make a clear point. You need people, Chancellors, or politicians that have the balls to stand up and say something-stand up and say something and be very clear.

**Nicholas:** Right. Right now, if we bring ourselves very contemporary, Germany is, whether it likes it or not, in a leadership position within Europe regarding the Euro Crisis. If someone watches this in a few years' time, the context currently is that the Greeks on the edge of defaulting precisely because Germany has been so successful and Germans have been so good at saving money, the Germans have got all the money. All the others are dependent on Germany to bail them out which pushes Germany into a leadership position. Obviously, a lot of the reason why the European Union has been as it is, is because people wanted to tie Germany down to stop Germany dominating Europe. It's a way of tying down the giant.

Adrian, how can Germany step into that leadership position in a really positive and helpful way to lead Europe out of the current crisis?

**Adrian:** Another easy question, I guess!

**Nicholas:** Just a small one.

**Adrian:** Just a small one. First of all, the crisis with the Euro, it's something that, for me, relates very much to European identity. That's also really a topic of Western Civilization. The currency system that we have right now, currency in itself, is obviously an agreement. You make agreements and it's built on trust and relationships.

In the crisis we have right now and we're facing in the financial market, they have just too much freedom to do everything they want. They just play casino with it on a very simplistic level. Another part is that, and that relates to the leadership perspective, Europe started as a monetary system and really moved forward in that kind of agreement on an economic level. We really failed to deal with the shadow elements of the culture. They are connected to Germany. They also connected to Europe, the idea that Jews are bad, that we should get rid of the Jews was not just a German issue at that time, the nationalism and all of it.

It was really like Europe has grown up. We had so many wars and fights and then to have something like the European Union is something so amazing. There wasn't much internal work. Again, as you said, if you don't trust and if you're afraid if Germany gets into a leadership position then you will work against this. In the end, Germany has to take a leadership perspective.

On the exterior financial market situation where you just fix the system and you're not getting to the roots of the system and addressing the roots of the system. That's a real challenge because if you just fix a system on the surface, it won't work. You just get into the same circle again. That happened with the financial markets.

In Germany, after the first financial crisis, there has been a lot of initiatives and a lot of work together with the sectors. For example, the three societal sectors like economic, civil society, and politics. That's something I would stress, that this could be a way to move forward. If you're able to generate a certain level of trust in those different sectors on a European level and then you find out what do we really need on a systemic level in the financial market.

How does the money serve us not how do we serve the money and the finance markets? How does the financial market serve us? This is often something I'm afraid that is not addressed or not seen. I'm not a politician. It's very difficult to say where can you enter, where's the entry points. Again, it comes down to really people in leadership positions that have a certain sense of their own and a certain sense of consciousness who are able to see the bigger picture in addressing those issues.

**Nicholas:** Finally, I'm British. I've done some thinking in that work with the German Government on the British-German relationship. I just wonder, what's your perspective on that? What's the relationship between Britain and Germany?

**Adrian:** The relationship between Britain and Germany. When I think about Great Britain, I have a certain sense of ... to be honest with you, I have a certain sense of a healthy rules, structures, law, government, order, this kind of royalty that got carried on in the Commonwealth, royalty. I have still a strong sense or still a strong feeling of this culture, this very sophisticated culture that, in a certain way, dominated almost half of the world in a certain time.

There's a certain ease. There's a certain smartness that comes to mind on one level and then, more contemporary, I was thinking about Britain and Great Britain or London, there's so much diversity of course, you have also difficulties. You really did a lot of work on intercultural exchange and what you would call multiculturalism or what you could call the challenge. You face a lot of challenges on how to integrate people from all over the world and to develop this kind of culture.

This is something I would see Britain being on the forefront and pushing that further as well. Of course, you're an island. You are, in a certain way, isolated and took a step back from Europe with the whole financial crisis. I hope that it won't be this isolated because we need the British, in a certain way, the British tradition or the British thinking for Europe. We really need that. Also, we need Britain as the connection between Europe and the States. This is also a very important role of the British people or the British identity could play an important role.

**Nicholas:** Great. Adrian, it has been absolutely fascinating talking to you. I wonder, right at the very end, having got all that off your chest, what is your highest vision for Western Civilization or global Civilization? Who are we? Where are we going?

**Adrian:** The beauty of Western Civilization, "Who are we?" is, for me, we're the pioneer in something what I would call modernity. We really moved forward the period of enlightenment. We are part of it. Of course, now, there are coming competing modernities all over the place but they're really looking to us. They're really seeing, "What did they do? What have they done wrong? What did they have that's good?"

I really like the idea of enlightenment and modernity. I really would like to see the Western societies coming together celebrating that and really doing their work and they have already done their work on learning out of the mistakes we have done and out of the shadows we have, integrate them, and then really move forward to this vision of developing something like global culture. Not just Western but a global culture.

The Western mind is very much focused on thinking. You could say just get rid of thinking and orient yourself more into being. For me, personally, that's too easy. That won't work. How do we develop a thinking that is alive, creative and cooperates as well as the intuitive perspective? This is, for me, integral theory or integral practice.

This is something that has really grown out of the Western tradition. Not just the Western tradition but a lot of it, from my perspective, has grown out of the Western tradition, connected to it. If you can move this forward, celebrate it, and integrate it, bring our ideas more into life and into reality, this would be quite amazing.

Use the wealth that we have to serve this higher purpose of developing a healthy global start of a revolution. It sounds a bit funky but that's what I could see. For me, this is also the question of the next generation, that they really get this sense of global identity without missing out the nationalistic ... not nationalistic but the national identity part because, then, they'll be really ... still a long way to go, 150 years maybe but we're going to get there. I truly believe that we're going to get there.

**Nicholas:** Fantastic, Adrian. If anybody would like to get in touch with you, how would they all read your writings? How would they do that?

**Adrian:** On the writings, you have to know German but you can always connect me on Facebook. Send me a message over Facebook. You'll find me as Adrian Wagner, or you just send an e-mail at my e-mail address and I will give it to you so you can put it in. It's adrian.wagner@lebensfieber.de

I'm open and I'm looking forward to hear from people that are interested and want to engage and do something together. I'm looking forward to keep the conversations going. It's a very important conversation. I'm very thankful that you have put out this topic and this video. It's a good work that needs to be done, I think.

**Nicholas:** Thanks, Adrian.

**Adrian:** Okay.

# Compassionate Healthcare

Re-humanising Medicine

**Dr Robin Youngson interviewed by Dr Nicholas Beecroft**
Dr Robin Youngson is an anesthesiologist trained in the UK and practicing in New Zealand for the last twenty years. Robin is an inspiring visionary and catalyst for truly compassionate, holistic, mindful and healing healthcare. Through opening himself and his own personal journey to others, he touches the heart of patients, healthcare professionals and hospital managers. As founder of Hearts in Healthcare and author of "TIME TO CARE-How to love your patients and your job," he is a powerful advocate for the transformation of healthcare.

In this interview, he draws on his frustrating experience of trying to get proper care for his daughter who had been seriously injured and admitted to his own hospital for 100 days. Within a few hours he went from being a senior doctor, a powerful person in that hospital system, to a disempowered advocate for good care. He describes his own journey from doctor as technician to doctor as a mindful, healer and compassionate human being.

Robin shares some of the evidence for holistic, compassionate healthcare and gives examples of where this is already happening. He discusses how he benefitted from taking a mindful approach to his own thoughts, feelings and behaviors and how that radically transformed the healthcare experience for his patients, colleagues and himself. He talks about burnout and cynicism in medical staff. He shares his challenges in trying to reform the healthcare system.

He has realized after 15 years of trying that there is no point in trying to persuade people or systems to practice compassionate healthcare. Instead, he has founded a global network of early adopters, passionate advocates and practitioners of caring, healing, holistic healthcare called Hearts in Healthcare. The network enables the sharing of powerful inspiring stories, of good evidence, of techniques that work and experience in transformational change.

Robin is married with three grown-up children and two grandchildren. An unassuming overachiever, Robin Youngson was born in the UK in 1955. Starting life as an Army child, he followed his family to postings throughout the British Empire before experiencing the horrors of institutional life in an English boarding school. In 1977 he graduated from Cambridge University with a degree in engineering, and worked for three years in the highly hazardous field of oil exploration to pay his way through medical school.

Robin has combined clinical practice with many leadership roles in healthcare. He was a founding member of the national Quality Improvement Committee in New Zealand and also advised the World Health Organization on strategies for patient safety and putting people at the center of healthcare. As a practicing anesthesiologist, Robin has for years been a lone voice on the international speaking circuit for compassionate, whole patient care.

He is the founder of the international HEARTS in HEALTHCARE movement launched in 2012.

**Nicholas:** Robin Youngson, welcome to the series, "Exploring the Future of Western Civilization."

**Robin:** Alright. It's a great pleasure to talk with you, Nicholas.

**Nicholas:** A bit of background about Robin. I met him I think about four years ago when he was giving a talk in London about compassion in healthcare. He's an anesthetist, originally from England, but for many years living in New Zealand, and he's really a really inspiring doctor. He's someone who's gone through a real change in his own life with lots of experiences which have made him passionate about changing the way that we do medicine and healthcare to make it really caring and compassionate.

He's founder of the global organization, Hearts in Healthcare, which is a social movement that is helping to draw people together all over the world who are passionate about making healthcare really healing and compassionate based on the staff and the patients. He started off as an engineer but very quickly realized his vocation in medicine. Since coming into medicine, he's had many, both clinical and leadership, roles.

He was a founding member of the National Quality Improvement Committee in New Zealand and he was also the New Zealand representative on the World Health Organization International Steering Committee for Patient Safety Solutions. He helped launch the World Health Organization strategy for people at the Center of Healthcare. He's currently an honorary senior lecturer at Auckland University and, most recently, launched this book summarizing all of his inspirational work called, "Time to Care: How to Love Your Patients and Your Job." So, welcome, Robin.

**Robin:** Thank you. One of the advantages of being in a small country like New Zealand with a population of only four million. What my father describes as being a big fish in a small pond.

**Nicholas:** Yes.

**Robin:** We shouldn't be too impressed with all of that.

**Nicholas:** Do you mind if we start with a very personal introduction, because I think it would be really good if people could hear your own journey from the way you used to do medicine and what changed you, what opened your eyes.

**Robin:** Yes, I guess it has been a long journey. When I was a Senior House Officer (Junior Doctor) in England coin anesthetics, I actually managed to write and publish a book, a handbook for surgical patients. For a very long time I've been interested in kind of trying to promote the patient's rights and give them information. And as I found as a junior doctor in the UK, I spent an awful lot of time explaining to patients what it was all about. A lot of fear comes from the unknown. I think the thing in leadership roles and working with indigenous people of New Zealand and managing many challenging situations kind of broadened my outlook about healthcare and medicine.

Certainly a milestone for me was in 2004 when our 18 year old daughter, Chloe, was driving to university and unaccountably crossed the center line on a blind corner and met a big truck coming the other way and was in one of those awful car wrecks that you see on the TV or the newspaper where you cannot recognize at all what kind of a car it is. They'd cut the roof off. Meredith, my wife, and I got the phone call from the police to say that our daughter was very severely injured and was on her way to the hospital, and we rushed to a major teaching hospital here in New Zealand to wait anxiously for a long time.

As it turned out, her sole major injury was a very unstable fracture of C1, C2 in her neck, grossly unstable. So all the emergency services did a great job of pulling her out without doing her harm, and her spinal cord was bruised but pretty intact. But as a consequence of the severity of that injury, it was decided that she would be treated conservatively and she lay in bed for three months flat on her back with a steel halo screwed into her skull and her head completely immobilized and able only to see the ceiling of the room that she was in, in a major hospital, in fact, the biggest hospital in New Zealand, and a big flashy hospital. It was a lovely place to be.

She was there for exactly a hundred days, a hundred nights. I must, I mean I had worked in that hospital as a senior specialist, as an anesthetist, and was very familiar with it. I knew the surgeon who was looking after her and I had a lot of faith in him, her spinal surgeon, and we would make the judgment that the quality of the technical care, generally speaking, was very good. There were mistakes and errors that are inevitable if you spend three months in hospital. It was really the lack of attention to some other aspects of her health and wellbeing that caused us really grave concern.

The first thing was that here's an intelligent 18 year old, a university student, who's tied down to her bed with her head immobilized so that the only thing that she can see is the ceiling. So she can't see people who come into the room unless they lean right over her. She can't see out the window. She cannot see a television. She can't read a book or a magazine, and she has a requirement for something to sustain her psychological and emotional wellbeing for three months, because if you did that to a person in Abu Ghraib prison, you'd be sent to jail for a long time. (laughter)

So we became sometimes surprised when it became apparent that in this very large hospital in a major city, they simply had no services at all to provide disability support and aids to an inpatient, that all the services were applied to their outpatients. So we begged and asked the occupational therapist to come and do assessment of her disability and her daily needs of living and all those kinds of her things. We asked, "Is that your role?" She said, "Yes, exactly." But the priorities on that service were such that at no time in the hundred days did she ever get an Occupational Therapy assessment. After …

**Nicholas:** By the way, Robin, at that time you were a senior doctor in this hospital?

**Robin:** Yes, well actually, I had subsequently left that hospital, but I'd been a senior specialist in that hospital and indeed I'd been on the Executive Management Committee. I had been the Clinical Director of Healthcare Improvement in that whole organization. So I knew the Chief Executive, I knew all the managers and the senior doctors. So I was a powerful and influential person within that system. In fact, I was there every day that Chloe was there and the receptionist on the front desk thought that I still worked there, because I went past every day and they knew my face and they waved and said, "Hi, Robin."

So after two weeks, we finally got our first disability aid which is a mirror on a swivel in a position which she could reach with her one good arm that she could use. She could twist it around and get some view of who was coming into the room or the view out the window. That proved to be the only disability aid that she was provided for in three months of a hospital stay. She couldn't see a television or read a book and after asking and begging, trying to persuade and when a loved one is critically injured and completely at the mercy of a hospital system, you're very circumspect about the way that you interact with that.

You don't piss people off, you try to keep them on one side and be nice to them and appreciative, but eventually after about a month of frustration I realized that we weren't making progress. So I went ahead and bought a widescreen laptop computer and I built a frame to suspend it above her bed. Then I asked for an internet connection. There was a network connection on the bed head right behind her and I knew this would connect to the internet. So I phoned up the hospital computer department and explained that my 18 year old daughter had a broken neck and was severely disabled and this was her connection to the outside world, and of profound importance, and that if she could have web access and email and so on, that would just make a profound difference to watching TV.

They explained to me all the reasons why that couldn't be possible and I think I nearly started crying and I said, "Well, please try to imagine this is your daughter and what would you do for her." And they weren't going to budge. So I said, "Well, okay, I'm just going to buy a wireless internet connection and install that in the hospital." They said, "If you come and do that, we'll come and remove it, because it's against hospital policy." It kind of went on like this.

That's the only time I pulled strings. It turned out that the Chief Medical Officer was one of my colleagues an anesthetic specialist, so phoned him up and one hour later I had the general manager of information systems in Chloe's hospital room saying, "Well, of course we can do this. It's trivial. We can get it fixed up in an hour." It turns out in the hospital that we have an extremely efficient system to deliver a meal tray into a patient's room and take it away an hour later. You notice there's something missing in that account. That is there's absolutely no reliable means of ensuring that that food gets into the patient, and anyway the food has such poor nutritional value. I think we spend about a pound per patient per day on the hospital food, and it's completely impossible to provide nutritious food that will be healing for patients.

I mean, she had many broken bones and injuries and it was really crucial for her survival and her healing and getting out of hospital that she had good quality nutrition. So it became apparent that a) she wasn't going to get fed at all and she'd just be left hungry and b) the food was awful and such poor nutritional value that my wife, Meredith, and Chloe's sisters and friends put together a roster so we were there at the hospital twice a day every day to ensure that she was fed tasty, nutritious food. That cost us more than a thousand dollars in car parking charges for the privilege of ensuring that our daughter just had the food she needed to recover.

Now, we'd really began to get a sense that even in this top Teaching Hospital where the technical quality care was good, there were really basic human needs not being met at all. Really distressing.

**Nicholas:** That's with you as a senior doctor. So if it's like that for you, what would it be like for someone who was unassertive and fearful and not very self-confident?

**Robin:** Very much the case. In the room there was a poor Maori teen-age boy with multiple fractures, tied in bed in traction. His family simply didn't come to visit at all. I mean, they couldn't afford it. They didn't have a car and it was three bus fares and the kids were at school, and he was just left to fend for himself. We were deeply fearful for those who didn't have an advocate within the system.

One of the things that caused us awful distress; one day she had ex-tremely severe pain from bladder spasm. She had some spinal cord injury and this was causing her a lot of trouble. There's a sophisticated acute pain team in this large hospital and they'd been to visit her and they made a very good four point plan to relieve her pain. If point one doesn't work, try point two, and so on in a stepwise plan. Well, step one didn't work at all. Step two was very simple, it was just to put some local anesthetic, some lignocaine in her urinary catheter into the blad-der to try to anesthetize the bladder and to stop the spasms and she was getting kind of eight out of ten pain.

When you're lying in bed with your head immobilized with a broken neck, it's really hard to kind of express your distress and your pain and you can't have a real paddy, you can't throw things. So it was extremely distressing to watch. We called a nurse and said, "Well step one didn't work, please can you try step two, which is written in the plan" and all we had to do was to get some lignocaine and put it in her catheter. The nurse said, "I'm not really happy to do that. I've not seen it done be-fore," and I said, "Well, please can you ask the charge nurse?"

So the Charge Nurse came and said, "Well, I'm not really familiar with that and I'm not really happy to do it. We'll have to get the House Sur-geon." So I said, "Please call the House Surgeon." We paged him and he was busy and he wouldn't come. Then we paged him and he was still busy and wouldn't come, and this went on for hours, and Chloe was just weeping in distress and severe pain and the whole family was there and we were just all crying and the nurses became very embarrassed and felt very inadequate and started hiding from us, because they knew that Chloe was in severe pain and they felt really incapable of doing anything about it and the Charge Nurse wasn't helping and the House Officer wasn't helping.

So eventually I went to the nurse's station. I said, "Okay, I want you to call the Registrar now. I want you to do it now. This is intolerable." So they made a phone call and I thought, "Thank God, help is coming." So the Duty Nurse Manager arrived and I thought, "Great, here's a really senior nurse who will be able to sort this out." She took me aside and he said, "Doctor Youngson, I'm going to ask you to stop behaving like that, you are making the nurses feel threatened." At which point I think I nearly started crying and I said, "I thought you'd come to help Chloe." I think probably I had tears in my eyes.

At which point I thought, "This is ridiculous." I went straight to the phone, phoned the switchboard and said, "Get me the on-call anesthetist," and that wonderful registrar with whom I'd previously worked arrived within only a few minutes, and in two minutes completely abolished the pain. It's a day that will live with us forever. I don't think there's much that's more distressing than seeing a loved one in terrible pain and distress, sitting in the middle of a big hospital where everything that's needed to relieve that pain is immediately available and nobody will respond to that. Just nobody. Even to someone like myself who is influential and powerful in the system.

So, yes, those were, I guess, those were pretty informative experiences for us. It made us realize that even though there were lots of very caring and compassionate nurses and doctors, somehow the way the whole system fits together was just really callous to Chloe's needs. That really was ... that became a point of no return. At that point, I said, "Okay, now we're going to do a campaign to change the system. Whatever we have to do, there's no choice anymore." And that was six years ago.

**Nicholas:** Many people respond to that, by saying, "All doctors and nurses are bad" or "medicine is terrible, I wish it could all be run by alternative healthcare people," et cetera. But, of course, you are a doctor and, until recently, you've been this senior doctor in that very hospital, so you know what it's like sitting on the other side of the fence, so to speak.

**Robin:** Yes.

**Nicholas:** How did that affect you as a clinician?

**Robin:** I'm not sure that particular period of time made a lot of difference, because I'd been on a long journey already and for about 15 years I only did anesthetics part time and for the rest of the time I was in a variety of world leadership roles, some really challenging. I got involved in, for instance, conflict resolution and maternity services whether there was a complete breakdown of relationships between midwives and doctors and this was causing a great deal of harm to patient care and a lot of distress and distrust and escalating rates and interventions and the caesarian section rate going up and up and some poor outcomes.

I got involved in some very courageous work with a facilitator. We got all the parties involved in that including the senior obstetricians, pediatricians and anesthetists and midwives and locked them in a room and used role play and sociodrama. Can you imagine senior medical specialists doing that? (laughing) I don't think I'll ever seen anyone looking quite so scared. Some avoided eye contact, like going into the fetal position, head down, "I'm not going to get involved in this." By the end of the day we had people role playing those tense situations and doing reverse roles; doctors role playing midwives and patients and midwives. There was a very good midwife who just role-played a senior obstetrician and she just had all the manners and the arrogance and she did it really well. It's what Chris Argyris called double loop learning, where you're getting to dig underneath the assumptions that people have and the beliefs they have about each other, and expose those and that led to a monthly forum, in maternity, of dialogue where I agreed to facilitate the forum, where there is still a huge amount of conflict and difficulty and I had all my own hot buttons as an anesthetist. I agreed to do that with a facilitator sitting beside me and coaching me in real time.

So I did attempt to leave this forum and it would go off the rails and the facilitator will stop me and say,"Robin, I noticed this was happening and Judy, can I just check, do you feel as if the forum was hearing what you were trying to say?" "No, absolutely not." So, "Robin, I notice you were doing this, you were trying to shove it down, if you try this it might work better. Do you want to give it another go?" So I exposed myself to quite a bit of vulnerability to be coached in front of the whole forum and my peers. It was really cute, but the facilitator helped the forum for exactly nine months and on the nine month he said, "Well, I have made no intervention. You don't need me anymore. You've learned the skills of dialogue." That was kind of cute, because it was in maternity services. Over the course of two years, just by rebuilding our relationships be-tween all those different parties, our caesarean section rate fell by 30% and the clinical outcomes were transformed.

**Nicholas:** Really?

**Robin:** The patient complaints fell by a factor of three and the staffing went from crisis level to fully staffed.

**Nicholas:** Wow!

**Robin:** What I gained was self awareness. What I gained was the awareness that I actually have an impact on others; the kind of mindful-ness, the kind of approach, my behavior, has a really big influence on others, and I was being coached in real time about my behavior and how others perceived me. It began to change me pretty profoundly as a doctor. So there are a lot of experiences like that.

**Nicholas:** Can you describe that? What you mean?

**Robin:** Well, let's try to give an example. In a hospital where I worked for a long time, there were no junior doctors. It was a busy maternity unit and there were consultant obstetricians and anesthetist residents on duty doing 24-hour shifts, seven days a week.

So as an anaesthetic specialist, I might have a really busy day and do a few caesarian sections during the day and be called back and forth and finally get home at 10 o'clock and have a late dinner and go to bed at midnight and get called out at 1 o'clock for an epidural and back to bed and called out at 2 o'clock for anesthesia, back to bed at 4 and called out at quarter past 4 for another epidural. There were times when, really, I began to get pretty sorry for myself and kind of grumpy.

When I was driving into the hospital, I'd be thinking, "That stupid midwife, why couldn't she call me when I was already in the hospital? I was there just 15 minutes ago, and she's called me. I just got back to bed and taken my clothes off, my head's set on the pillow, and I just fallen asleep, and she phones me again." So there's a fair amount of bringing grumpiness and ill temper into the encounter, which is not what a mother needs when she's very vulnerable, in severe pain and labor.

There was a wonderful patient I had who really taught me about the power of choosing an attitude. One day driving to the hospital becoming much more aware of kind of my own thoughts and attitudes and how I respond to others. I suddenly felt ashamed in the middle of this drive that here I was being very grumpy and sorry for myself when I was being invited to really a remarkably intimate event. Childbirth is about one of the most intimate things that happens in our human life, and to be called in to be a part of that, just seeing a mother very vulnerable, sometimes completely stark naked, in a lot of pain, fearful. I just became aware that the quality of spirit that I brought into that room would have a very material effect on the outcome.

So that developing self-awareness made me take a choice, which is to choose an attitude and just able, when I'm driving in the middle of the night, I'm not going to waste my energy on these foolish thoughts about feeling sorry for myself and grumpy and tired, and I actually reflect purposely on the extraordinary privilege of that invitation. When I get to the door I'll pause for a minute and I'll try to collect myself and try to bring some compassion and kindness and gentleness into that room where things are pretty stressful. And I notice very quickly that had a really major effect on what was going on, so ...

146

**Nicholas:** What effect did it have?

**Robin:** Well, one effect that it had is that a lot of the grumpy midwives appeared to have a personality transplant. When the anesthetist is being called into a room to do an epidural, that wasn't in the birth plan at all. It was an eight page plan about natural things and breathing and no pain and how wonderful childbirth is going to be. Then this mother's decided that she really hurts, and she wants an epidural and the independent midwife is not really in favor of that.

So sometimes coming into the room I felt like the devil, and I was not greeted warmly. It was an uphill struggle to get it done, and it would take me ages to get the mother positioned and find the equipment. After I'd chosen a different attitude and come into the room with a different attitude, for a few months I noticed that when I came in the room I might be greeted warmly, and I had the sense that my praises had been sung before I got there and the mother was already immaculately positioned to do the epidural. The equipment was there, and I got it done in about three minutes flat and the midwife would greet me warmly and introduce me to everyone and the quality of the pain relief was much better.

Over the years something really interesting happens, because in this particular hospital the obstetrician and the anesthetist were often on duty together. Every Tuesday for about seven years it was the two of us that provided care. One day I pulled all the data for a year, and I looked up the Caesarean section rate by the day of the week, and on the days that we were on duty the Caesar rate was half of the average. I mean, we were running at about a 13% Caesar rate, which is just extraordinary low.

**Nicholas:** Wow!

**Robin:** The obstetrician I worked with, a wonderful doctor, he had a similar philosophy, and I just became more and more aware that the quality of thoughts in my mind, the quality of feelings, the intention, the spirit I brought to the encounter, that was having a really major effect on important clinical outcomes. So there were lots of experiences that, over many years, that sensitized me to that.

**Nicholas:** Robin, you changed your own practice, and that's evolved in this way, but of course, you've taken on leadership roles and through your different leadership roles in hospitals, you've tried to change the culture and inspire others to follow your path. How has that been?

**Robin:** Well, you shouldn't forget that I was an engineer first and then a doctor. So I guess I had a pretty rationalist kind of approach. I was right into patient safety and understanding systems and so on. I worked for very many years on executive management teams and on national committees and with the World Health Organization. Some of that work was on technical aspects of patient safety, but I was all the time trying to push an agenda that we need to fundamentally change healthcare because there are some really big problems. One is that we have a biomedical approach to health care where if you have an 80-year-old patient who's got six or seven or eight different diagnoses, which they generally do, their care is extraordinarily fragmented between the rheumatologist, the cardiologist, the endocrinologist, the respiratory physician and so on.

It's as if there's not actually a doctor that sees the whole person, so it's very reductionist, particularly with the push of evidence-based medicine, more and more we don't treat the person with the illness, we're just treating disease X needs treatment Y. As the experience of Chloe showed, we're very much ignoring the emotional and psychological and spiritual aspects of care, and we have this very mechanical, reductionist kind of focus on caring. I've just learned more and more that there's a profound amount of harm, not only to patients, but also to doctors. I think it took me 14 years from day one at Med School to being appointed as a consultant anesthetist, that was a very big investment. In my early career, a lot of my self-esteem and self-identity was around technical expertise, and I certainly did not have the kind of human qualities and abilities to relate to people.

That's a very vulnerable position because, as a doctor, we meet many patients that we can't help, that we can't fix, that we can't cure, and worse still there are some patients we actually injure, we harm in the course of the treatment. And that left in me a really profound feeling of failure of professional purpose. If my whole role is around expertise and being really smart and training for so many years and being able to effect some cure and help people, I would go home feeling really pretty bad about myself when I couldn't do that. Yet I did not have the capacity to relate to that person as a human being. That's, I found in my experience, an extremely vulnerable place to be.

I can think of a number of patients that when things went badly, I just felt so inadequate that I just abandoned those patients. I never went to see them again. I didn't offer apology or explanation or support. They were just kind of left within the system because I felt really profoundly inadequate. What's joyous now is that with the skills and the capacity to make a human connection and to look after a whole human being, you never have to say, "Listen, I'm sorry. There's nothing I can do." There's a world you can do.

I've learned, particularly researching my book, I've become much more humble about what we do as doctors. We think that we fix and cure patients, but actually the healing occurs within the patient. We never mend a broken bone, we just set it straight and the body heals it. When a GI surgeon stitches a bowel back together, he doesn't fix the bowel. I mean, there are all these holes around it between the stitches, and the bowel heals itself together. If you look at the research around the capacity of human beings to heal themselves, the placebo effect seems to have an efficacy that's about equal to most of the medicines we use and, in some instances, a lot better.

**Nicholas:** What is the mechanism of healing? How does it work?

**Robin:** Very, very many mechanisms. I mean, in the beginning there was a kind of mechanical explanation on this which we called psychoneuro-immunology, and it's something that's part of it. For instance, there is a study, if you take a bunch of a hundred medical students and you give them a psychological questionnaire and you measure the quality of their thinking, some are quite optimistic and have more positive thinking, and some are anxious and pessimistic on the other side.

So if you divide them into two groups, the optimists and the pessimists, and then, I'm not sure this is ethical, but it's actually been done, you inoculate every single medical student with influenza A virus into the naso-pharynx, the standardized dose, and guess what, the clinical infection rate of the pessimists is three times higher than the optimists. There are many other studies like that. Survivors of heart attack where the pessimists, the negative thinkers, had a mortality rate three or four times higher than the optimists. So I think there are lots of mechanisms. Certainly, these are telling us that the immune system is profoundly affected by our thoughts and our emotions, our whole autonomic nervous system.

There are just lots of mechanisms. The power of human touch is remarkable, and if I could reach through this screen and put my hand close to you, and if we put an ECG, lead on my heartbeat and an EEG lead on your skull, we'd be able to demonstrate that some of your brain cells are now firing off in synchrony with my heartbeat and vice versa.

So there's an electromagnetic field that's influencing people around us and changing physiology. The research on therapeutic touch, this is a modality of treatment where you're holding your hands close to the patient without stopping them. I mean, even on premature neonates, who certainly don't understand or have the conscious awareness of what's going on, there are pretty profound changes in their physiology, their autonomic function, not the least important differences in outcome like length of stay and complication rate.

So I don't think that we understand all of the mechanisms, but it seems pretty clear that human consciousness does not end where your skin is. There's a field of energy or information that extends further than that.

**Nicholas:** Yes.

**Robin:** There's now a whole new science called interpersonal neurobiology that, as we are talking on this interview, you've got big, specialized neurons called mirror neurons that are looking at my facial expression and body language and so on. It's like we have a broadband internet connection between our nervous systems. In the relationship between a mother and child, that is actually two-way influencing the neurodevelopment, that influences the creation of synapses, of creating new neurons, of strengthening parts of the brain, our autonomic nervous system, the whole endocrine system. It's just the relationship between human beings profoundly changes each other's physiology. That's extremely easy to measure.

So there are just lots of influences we have on each other. At medical school I was taught this high ideal of clinical detachment for two reasons. One is that the theory was that if you weren't objective and detached, you couldn't make good decisions. You couldn't really see the patient clearly. The second was that because we see, as doctors, so much suffering and loss that if we had an emotional connection with patients that we would simply burn out.

Well, the neuroscience is telling us that clinical detachment doesn't exist. It's the strange Western idea, this dualism between mind, cognition and emotion. I mean, in the Tibetan Buddhist culture they don't even have a word for emotion. You can't translate that English word, because every concept they have of mental states combines thinking, cognition, and emotion as one inseparable whole. It's only in the Western world we have this idea that they're somehow separate.

**Nicholas:** I remember at medical school being taught to cut off and be so-called objective, but you're saying that that's just a trick of the mind, and in fact, the body and the spirit are still very much connected to the patient, and we're just pretending to disconnect.

**Robin:** Yes, we are. That's very harmful to patients. I mean, it just strikes cold fear into the heart of patients, because they don't have time for detachment.

**Nicholas:** Yes.

**Robin:** We don't either, but we pretend that we do.

**Nicholas:** One Christmas I went to stay with a friend who is an orthopedic surgeon, and to my horror, he woke me up at six in the morning on a Saturday to go to his ward round. I hadn't been on an orthopedic ward round since I was at medical school 15 years earlier. I found it fascinating. He's a friend. I have a extremely high regard for him.

I know he's a really good doctor, as doctors go, and hugely caring in his life in general, much more than the average person.

We went round about 15 patients, and about half of them were regulars. So they were over just sitting there, on their iPad or just watching telly and didn't really pay much attention. The other half were fresh cases who had never been in the hospital, and often, they were people who came in the emergency. Without exception, I could see they were absolutely terrified, really scared. "What the hell am I doing here? I'm in a lot of pain, very scared about what's going to happen to me. I want to know what my options are, what's there," blah, blah, blah. Just physically, I can see each person was terrified, and bursting with questions.

My friend's body language was very much standing over them, talking loudly. "Hello! How are you? Good morning." It was almost as if he put his hand in their face and, "Shut up. I'm not going to talk to you. I'm just going to talk loudly over you like this." Really, he wanted to know about two questions, like have they got a temperature and are they conscious. From a clinical point of view, they were basic postoperative questions. Finally, when we were driving home after about an hour and a half, I realized what I was going to say that's quite sensitive because it was a criticism, but I sort of said, as delicately as I could, "I noticed just how scared those people were. I think they probably had a lot of questions for you."

He didn't bite my head off, but he instantly knew what I was saying and he said, "Look, I work in this hospital every day from about 8 in the morning until 8 in the evening. This is a Saturday, it's my weekend. It's the only time I get to spend with my family. If I gave all of those people the time that they wanted, each of them would want half an hour of my time and I'd be finished. I wouldn't have any time with my family, I would burn out, and it just isn't possible to do medicine that way." I didn't really have an answer for that. What would you say?

**Robin:** Well, I've made an observation from this and noticed that the evidence is really clear. You can test it in the laboratory. You can take human beings, even make a standardized incision in their arm and you can measure how many days it takes to heal. If you deliberately stress those people with a variety of the sort of things they do in psychological experiments or if you put them in a supportive environment, there's about a two to one difference in the number of days it takes for that wound to heal. So those frightened patients are absolutely and importantly delaying and impairing that wound healing, that's important.

The second thing is that they're also profoundly impairing their immune system so you would probably find, you could do a randomized controlled trial and compare stressed patients with patients that were comfortable you might find a very important difference in the incidence of surgical site infection.

When you think about the patient's emotions and psychological wellbeing actually, it is causing us a lot of extra complications in work and delay and down the track which we don't necessarily see. I think it would be very wrong to deny just how challenging is the work environment of most of the people that work in healthcare. There's a researcher in London called Jill Maben. She has a compelling interest in what happens to nurses during the early part of their career and she's followed nurses longitudinally from their last week as nursing students, when they graduate university with very high ideals of whole patient compassionate care into the first two or three years of practice in busy hospitals in the National Health Service in London.

She found that the overwhelming majority of those nurses, that their hopes and ideas were either compromised or actually crushed. That was the language she used. Among them were leaving their jobs, job-hopping or burning out. I think that is the reality. What intrigues me is that even in the most stressed hospitals and we certainly have them here in New Zealand, there is a greater difference between the quality of healthcare between big stressed city centre hospitals and quieter, more relaxed small town hospitals.

We have all of these very common stressors and difficulties in shortages of staff and funding cutbacks. What intrigues me is that within that disordered, chaotic stressed system with a lot of people burning out, there are some individuals that nurture each day with serenity and growth and happiness and a smile. It's really intriguing to observe because, they never hurried and they always seem to have time for the patient and they seem to be immune to a lot of the daily irritations and frustrations that annoy most of us.

I think really the key to this is appreciative inquiry and looking at what really works and what is it about these individuals that allows them to actually flourish within this disordered stressed system? There are many different elements to that. I've learned in my practice as an anesthetics specialist, if I'm doing a general anesthetics list, I have very few minutes to meet a patient and to build the report and to find the things that are important. I have learned to be much more skilled in making a connection with the patient and investing a little bit of time upfront.

In my early career I was just a specialist. I had no idea at all about the power relationship between a doctor and a patient. I was always nice and I was friendly and, "Hello, Mr. X, my name is Dr. Youngson, I'm an anesthesia specialist, come and sit down. Now, you're coming for a gall bladder operation next week and I see you have asthma. Tell me about your asthma." You have lost any opportunity to tell me at all about what's on your mind and what concerns you or what's really important. If you're really courageous, at the end of the consultation, I say, "You got any questions?" and you're very likely to say, "No." Or you might hesitate at the door and say, "Yeah, I was actually worried, because the last time I had an anaesthetic, I got woke halfway through in the middle of surgery and I was really worried about that." Or you might not tell me at all.

So I've got much more skilled at building a human connection and explaining to people who I am and what my role is and why we've come together, because most people that's seeing the specialist, they're just scared. They have no idea that I think something must be really wrong. I explain the process that we are going to go through, then I say, "It'd be really helpful for me to know what's on your mind? How are you feeling? Are there any worries?" Or things that are going round and round and you get payback time and time again.

So becoming more skilled in making connections, finding out what's important to people up front really saves a lot of time. I had a wonderful story from a staff nurse on a medical ward and she was nicknamed "The Angel" by all of the patients. At the beginning of the shift she would be allocated patients and she will get that number of face towels and she would moisten them. She will put them in the microwave oven and, a bit like on Singapore Airlines, she would go to each of the five or six patients and give them a hot tea towel and say, "My name is Julie, and I'm going to be your nurse today, and just give me an amount of your time and tell me what's on your mind and what I can do to make your day better."

She says it just saved her hours and hours of work, and there's really good evidence now from a formalized process like early rounding, because what happens is that the care has become so chaotic and fragmented and the nurse's call buzzer is going for the time. We have all got into reactionary mode and we are not mindful about what we're trying to do and how to achieve it.

So the evidence on early rounding for nurses, this is where the nurse director says, "Well, I know you're distressed and busy and you really don't have time, but on top of that we are going to ask you to go and see your patients every single hour and just check how they are. Do they need some pain relief, do they need to go to the toilet, is the water within reach? Can you make them more comfortable explaining what the plan of their care is and do that every hour?"

The evidence in that is really striking. When you do that, the number of call bells just dramatically goes down. The patients are greatly more satisfied. Complications like bed sores and patient falls, fall dramatically. You can put a pedometer on the nurse and show that she walks a mile and a half less per her shift on an eight-hour shift, than, before they change.

So when we turn chaotic, reactive care into mindful patient centered care that anticipates their need, then we create time. So those that move with grace, with serenity through the systems, their care is much more efficient and they create stillness around it. The other thing is that if I asked health professionals, "What is the greatest barrier to compassionate caring?", by far the commonest answer is, "We don't have time to care."

**Nicholas:** Yes.

**Robin:** That is by far the commonest answer. Yet, care and compassion just happens in magical moments. It doesn't take a lot of time. It doesn't take hours. When you have an intimate connection with a patient, when you're really paying attention and you bring an openhearted compassion, time stands still. Time only has this kind of linear mechanical kind of quality to it, when we're so focussed on tasks and when we focus on relationships and being present, then time just becomes dimensionless and you have this amazing moments of connection and healing that provides deep caring compassion.

I can think of stories like that on Chloe's first day in the hospital. We met three extraordinarily compassionate practitioners, and I can't tell these stories without getting emotional. I noticed these stories have seared into my memory and that will live with me forever, and they say, "If you're in a hospital for a while you'll never remember what was said to you or what happened, or the emotional experience of it. There was a wonderful transient care nurse. When you're critically injured you go from the trauma unit to the CT scanners to the operating theatre to the ICU, all these journeys. He anticipated the need for pain relief and got extra syringes and morphine when she's going for a CT scan with a broken neck, which was going to take a long time and the morphine was going to wear off. It's the tiniest things. On the journey to the CT scanner, you go between an old building and a new building and there's a metal strip along the floor. (choked with emotion) This wonderful nurse, mindful of the broken neck and she was in pain, she stopped the trolley and he lifted each wheel individually over the joint so that her broken neck wouldn't be jarred.

You can see in me the emotion that that creates, the memory of that. That took 30 seconds and those moments are for further healing. I mean, they just made us feel safe. When we teach people skills and teach them to be present and teach them to learn, most important for patients, care becomes much more efficient, much more effective, much more timely. We know now from positive psychology that the parts of wellbeing the simple acts of kindness, compassion, gratitude, appreciation serving others, that's what builds this happiness and wellbeing in resilience.

Those are the tiny acts of kindness, and when you make that a daily habit that simple daily habit of small kind acts from many health professionals is enough to reach a personal turning point where they go from being a stressed, burned out health professional to a happy, serene health professional that somehow always finds the time to care in exactly the same environment, and it's often transforming to health professionals. There are lots of stories from health professionals and lots of health professionals that are transforming themselves and finding resilience and wellbeing even within the stress system.

**Nicholas:** Most people do go into nursing or medicine and allied professions because they genuinely do care, and they might not be Mother Theresa, they want to get paid, they have ego needs and also some things like that. Fundamentally, the vast majority of people that I've met actually do care, really. Even if people are really caring, which most are, even if people really want to do their best for the patient, which most do, what can you do to change the system to enable people to do it? Even if you can't change the system, what can you do to survive a toxic system and still provide good healthcare?

**Robin:** That has been challenging me for about 15 or 30 years and I would have to admit that most of my times the change or system prove that formal authorities have been pretty futile and I did try pretty hard. As a specialist myself I found myself Director of Quality Improvement at a major teaching hospital. I ended up on a national committee advising the New Zealand Government on quality and safety in healthcare. I've worked with the World Health Organization. I lobbied all sorts of people and Ministers. All that time, I was trying to progress an agenda of humanizing compassionate care, and it just didn't register, or it just wasn't a priority.

In fact, even if you look at the framework of quality improvement, such as the Institute of Healthcare Improvement or within your own country, many other countries, there will be a quality framework with a number of dimensions of quality. Actually, extremely few countries even recognize care and compassion as a dimension of quality at all. I know they do in Scotland. That's one of the first countries that does. It's their number one dimension.

That's unusual. So it's really not on the agenda at all, and I certainly got very frustrated. I did have a more positive experience. I had an opportunity to be involved in the design and building and commissioning and opening of an entirely new hospital, about a two hundred bed hospital term with a new emergency department, acute medical services, coronary care and so on, to serve an underprivileged community.

This wasn't building a new building from an existing hospital. This is an entirely new acute services. This is very much going to be a trend because everywhere else in the world we're closing down small hospitals and they actually decided to build one in a city 10 or 15 minutes' drive from another very large hospital. I worked for seven years with an inspirational general manager and a wonderful director of nursing. Within that hospital, we certainly had tremendous opportunity to begin to change the culture and to create a safe and the healing environment for the work within it. We pioneer things like apology and open disclosure.

There was a terrible incident where a 17 year old mother having a caesarian section caught fire in the operating theatre and received severe burns from alcohol where it caught fire under her drapes. We were one of the first hospitals to really work alongside of the patient and her family, to apologize and to get a forensic investigator and to share a little of our findings with the patient's family and support the clinicians involved and five weeks later, we had the whole thing wrapped up and the hospital exonerated. That patient defends our reputation. She didn't sue us, she actually defends our reputation because she trusted us.

I did know that it helps to change the culture if you have a supportive management. What subsequently happened is when a new Chief Executive was appointed it was decided it was very bad news to have this small hospital rather autonomous with its own leadership team. We all just lost our jobs. My clinical leadership role, half of my income, half of my job was just abolished in a management structure and it was made a satellite of a bigger hospital across town which actually was a very troubled hospital with a lot of difficulties.

It was interesting that the staff turnover rate in the small hospital was running about 7% and the big hospital about 20% or 30% and yet the management didn't seem to be able to reflect, "There's something going on here that's really important, because it's very costly for us, costly for the bottom line, to have a very high staff turnover." We had something that's optimistic and that was really exciting to be able to create a very positive change for a lot of years, and then to have that kind of torn apart and in the end, with my failure to get this agenda on to the kind of national and international agenda. Eventually I began to think, well the problem is that we are not understanding our systems. I very much subscribe now to the Margaret Wheatley theory of live system change. Health care is an extremely complex interactive system. Nobody can control it. This idea that our managers have that if you divide an organization into a lot of little bits and specify precisely their performance and hold people accountable, that somehow you'll have a good system. The flaw of that is that one poor manager has got the budget for the hospital food and he screws that down and he doesn't realize that with all the malnourished patients the average length of stay is going to go up and be doubled and it's going to cost millions of dollars on the other end.

Actually, it's rather ironic, because with medicines' reductionist, fragmented approach to care, the human being is mirrored exactly by the manager's reductionist fragmented approach to running large organizations. I've now given that up after about 15 years of getting incredibly frustrated. I've now decided that we need an entirely different strategy and that to change the complex system like healthcare a different strategy is required and, what we're now doing is trying to support and launch an international social movement. I've completely given up trying to persuade anyone to change. It's just a waste of energy for 15 years.

Now, all that we do is that we're seeking around the whole world through doing interviews like this or whatever, we just want to find the 5 or 10 percent of health professional that just provide wonderfully compassionate whole personal care and to connect them together and just support them and to fund the next five percent that are a bit curious about it that might be willing to come and have a look and join our community and to learn some new practices.

What's wonderful about that is that from all the evidence in positive psychology, we can say the pathway to wellbeing and resilience and happiness for health professionals who have terrible rates of burnout is small acts of kindness, gratitude, appreciation, serving others. That's the path to wellbeing, happiness and resilience. There is really good evidence on that. That's exactly what we need to do to rehumanize healthcare. Here's a movement where we want to connect people together around the world and say, "Join this inspirational community and find ways you can take responsibility for changing you own practice," like the surgical friend that you described, by things like choosing an attitude, that's an incredible pathway to change the whole world around me. I thought that all these grumpy difficult midwives were a problem out there. That was an external problem. In the Western world we tend to figure out the problem. Actually, the system is not out there, it's here. We are the system. Really, the only way to change the world is to change yourself. That's really the only way to change the world.

We've given up trying to influence authority figures and we're going to work with people one at a time and we're going to offer them an invitation, "Come and join this inspirational community. Come and meet some wonderful nurses and doctors and students and patient advocates and others who have transformed their own lives who have seized back power, who can change the world all around them." Because each of us has this big bubble around us and when we change ourselves, all these difficult midwives had a personality transplant. They probably thought I had had a personality transplant too!

This grumpy doctor has suddenly changed. So that's our strategy just to use the early adopters and then in certain places in the world, the ground is fertile. We're going to get a community practice where a whole bunch of people who are really excited about this, work together to start to establish completely different norms of practice. When these communities of practice join together across the world, you get about 15% of the system, and the whole system will flip and it will change radically. Then the authority figures will say, "Of course, we've always said that's what we're here for."

Now, we're not going to ignore them completely, because if any Chief Executive or someone in charge of a committee or whatever this is "I'm excited about this, come and work with us," we'll be in there like a shot.

**Nicholas:** In our current culture, I assume it's similar in New Zealand, because you mentioned evidence-based medicine, wouldn't it be nice if we had evidence-based leadership? Evidence-based medicine is a wonderful idea; the idea that medicine should be based on the very best available knowledge. No one could possibly disagree with that, but the problem is the way in which it is actually carried out and the quality of that science and the actual things about which we actually know versus the huge list of things which come under the heading of intuition, experience, wisdom and the massive list of unknown unknowns. It doesn't work out as well as it should. What is the evidence-based in leadership terms and in clinical terms that compassionate patient-centered healthcare is the best approach?

**Robin:** Yeah, that's the question that has really exercised me, and researching for my new book Time to Care, I looked at that pretty carefully. I think the answer to that is the evidence is diffuse. I mean, there are many areas, but when you bring it together it's really compelling. There's really powerful evidence, that emotional and psychological factors in patients profoundly affect physical outcomes. So with heart attack survivors, the pessimists are four times the mortality rate of the optimist.

So there are many studies like that. Over all the evidence, if you kind of do a meta-analysis of these effects and the influence of emotional and psychological wellbeing on physical health outcomes is about as big as the difference between smokers and non-smokers. So you put a huge amount of effort into persuading people to stop smoking, but we don't have to do much to look after the whole person.

So that's one piece of evidence – a lot of evidence around organizational dynamics and leadership, and if you really look after your staff and provide a caring and compassionate work environment and do lots of little things to look after your staff, probably the best evidence for this is in the Magnet hospital movement, particularly in the States. That is a really powerful impact on patient mortality, on staff turnover, on patient safety, on patient falls, on lots of different measures, and if you want to persuade healthcare executives that they should be interested that in this modern healthcare age where there's really a deep crisis and healthcare shortages.

In the USA, 15% of nursing posts are vacant and in the small hospitals in New Zealand, they're just desperate trying to get doctors. The evidence shows that those organizations where the leadership is more transformational leadership and looking after the health and wellbeing of their staff, of really understanding what motivates health professionals and speaking through those things, talking about caring and compassionate care in the community and those kinds of things, looking after health and wellbeing, that very dramatically reduces your staff turnover. That cuts millions of dollars off your bottom line in terms of staff turnover. There's a whole pile of evidence about the health and wellbeing of health professionals who have very high rates of burnout. At any one time, about a third of the doctors are burning out. 60% of physicians say they'd dissuade their children from going into medicine, they think it's such a bum deal. There is really strong evidence that connecting to the root of your vocation and to well being is the key to sustaining your workforce.

So there is kind of diffuse evidence in lots of different aspects and when you put it together it's really compelling. Here's a really important study. One of the areas in which modern medicine actually provides wonderful culmination of scientific technical medicine and whole person care and compassionate caring, is actually palliative care. Here's a study out of the States of patients with unresectable lung cancer. The insurance company in the States said that they carried out an experiment. Normally what would happen is that they would come to the point where they say, "We no longer will insure you for all of your chemotherapy and your surgery, and you're just going to have palliative care."

But someone really enlightened said, "We are going to fund you both for aggressive medical treatment and for palliative care. You can make a choice whether you have one, or both, or whatever. And if you agree to that, please join us on a randomized controlled trial and we'll see what happen and compare palliative care with aggressive medical treatment-chemotherapy and surgery. So it's a well conducted randomized controlled trial with large numbers. The outcomes are amazing. The patients having the aggressive medical care-that's chemotherapy and surgery, 38% of them had symptoms of depression. They were not a happy lot of patients at all. In the patients having palliative care, it was 16%, I think, it was a tiny fraction. So on average, they were much happier. The costs of care were radically different. The patients, not surprisingly, having aggressive medical care it was many thousands of dollars more per hospital stay. What was really intriguing was the average length of survival of the patients having the aggressive medical care, the best that modern medicine can offer, the average survival was 8.9 months, and the patients having palliative care survived on average 12 or 13 months! So that's really good evidence.

And you know, Nicholas, that medicine is very slow to adopt the evidence that exists. We knew that thrombolysis could reduce mortality from myocardial infarction by 40% back in the 80s, and it took about 20 years for it really to come into established practice and we still miss it out sometimes. So there's a wealth of evidence. I'm not against evidence-based practice at all, I think we just need to bring the evidence that whole person compassionate care is dramatically better for patients. It improves patient safety, it improves patient satisfaction, you get better rates of healing, shorter length of stay, cheaper care and better outcomes, and you have a happy workforce. So that is evidence-based medicine.

**Nicholas:** Robin, where is this up and running? Where are they doing this? Obviously there are pockets, there are good clinicians everywhere and everyone does a good job some of the time, but are there beacons or centers of excellence?

**Robin:** There are an extremely small number of organizations really working on this. So there's the Schwartz Center in Boston in the States. There's the group in Edinburgh, the Leadership and Compassionate Care Project. They were given a million pounds by a benefactor, saying, "Put the heart back in nursing care." They've done some tremendous work. There's the King's Fund, you'll be aware of, the Point of Care Program. Now I'm starting to scrape the bottom of the barrel for those organizations around the world that are trying to lead this care. I mean that's four or five organizations in the whole world that has 60 million health professionals.

There are little pockets of just wonderful care. I only know of one system which probably are the leaders in this, and I think the reason for that is that they've taken an approach of appreciative inquiry, and that's at the Center for Appreciative Practice. That's at the University of Virginia in Charlottesville. They brought together the school of medicine, the school of nursing, the kind of academic medical center, and the health services foundation. They've now done a tremendous amount of work. They've engaged nearly 2,000 people in this program and they've worked with about 40 different groups and they're using appreciative inquiry to drive forward care.

They've published a wonderful book just in the last year about Appreciative Inquiry. In medicine and healthcare we're so focused on problems, so if you've got a target for getting patients through your ER in four hours or six hours, whatever it is, typically you would bring all the doctors and nurses and clerks and orderlies together and say, "Well, how are we going to improve this?" Everyone will just order their problems and difficulties and they'll blame everyone else and they'll say, "Well, we did a wonderful job, and if the wards would only take our patients, if X-ray would do it quicker," and so on.

Appreciative inquiry is a very different approach. With the same group of people you say, "Tell us about, first of all tell us about the hopes and aspirations that brought you into healthcare?" and people would talk about caring, compassion and so on. Then they say, "Well, tell us about day when the emergency department just worked exceptionally well, when things ran so smoothly and when everyone worked as a team and things flowed well."

Tell us that story and how did that happen and what were the conditions that allowed that to happen?" That's called appreciative inquiry, and that radically changes the atmosphere in a room. You get very diverse groups of participants working together. The psychologists say that when we're stuck in a problem, in a rut, our whole perceptual system closes down and our imagination or creativity closes down, yet when we're in a positive frame of mind, our positivity, our creativity, our ability to problem-solve opens up. So they published a book called Appreciative Inquiry in Healthcare. This is the first major application of Appreciative Inquiry in healthcare. I want to read to you some of the chapter headings because you'll get a great sense of how profound this is. The first chapter is, "Keeping the Patient at the Heart of All We Do." "Helping Patients Deal With Loss and Transition." "Offering Hope and Healing." "Fostering Patients' Health." "Working Together in Teams." "Caring for Their Caregivers." "Experiencing The Awe and Wonder of Our Jobs."

This entire book is just full of questions. So I reckon probably they're the world leaders. The most senior doctor involved in this, it's very interesting, saying what a different job this is. He's a Professor of Medicine. He's also a director of the Mindfulness Center, so he's really interested in how we bring mindfulness and so on to our practice. He also teaches on a program called The Healer's Art and he's the director of The Physician Wellbeing.

So here we have this integration, here's really good evidence, here's one man, that's saying that compassionate caring is profoundly interrelated with physician wellbeing and with mindfulness and with the healer's art. I haven't had a chance to visit yet, but I reckon probably they're the world leaders in this and I profoundly and wonderfully commend this work.

Appreciative Inquiry in Healthcare is just great. It's the only one of its kind and if you want to get a really good successful strategy then read that book.

**Nicholas:** I remember at Medical School it being taught about the placebo effect, the effect the giving a blank pill, and the way in which you can maximize that, and I remember learning about the therapist effect, the power of the healer, whether it's the white coat or the doctor's authority, or the healing touch of the nurse and so on. But then haven't heard much about it ever since. It strikes me as odd that we don't give it very much thought. We could learn from a couple of groups. A lot of people in the alternative health arena, where they call themselves holistic practitioners and so on, often many of those can be quite hostile to medicine, and anti-medical.

There's like what I consider to be a false polarity between traditional medicine and alternative medicine, which it should be, we should want the best medicine, whatever that happens to be. I wonder what we've got to learn from them, because they've been quite good at maintaining the things that we've given up, like good bedside manner and compassionate care. Also, the other group is witch doctors or shamen. When we've sterilized medicine into a very sort of pseudo-technical profession, pretending it's all very technical and all about numbers and spreadsheets, we've neglected that deep, powerful, magical, spiritual connection. How can we learn from all of those people to do it well?

**Robin:** Yeah, a lot of that you've talked about in your question is what I call the meaning response, and that's not my original term. There's a wonderful paper called "Deconstructing the Placebo Effect and the Meaning Response" and that's most intriguing. It looked at lots of studies that examine the placebo effect and how powerful that can be, and he did an analysis of about 80 or a hundred randomized controlled trials of H2 receptor antagonists in the treatment of peptic ulcer disease. In that paper there's a scatter diagram where on one access is the healing rate for the control group and the other access is the healing rate for the treatment group, and there's a dot, which is for each study.

So it's a kind of a scattergram, a big cloud, and some studies have really low healing rates and some had high healing rates. What he observed is that there's really quite a strong correlation between the two arms, so that those studies that had a high healing rate for the drug trial, the active side of it, had a higher healing rate for the placebo arm also. He said, "Is this a difference in genetics? How do we explain this? His explanation is that in those trials in which all those factors you talked about-the authority of the physician, the white coat, the trust they had with the patients and whatever, that those trials in which the doctors, or the scientists, conveyed powerful meaning and healing in the efficacy of this drug had very high rates of healing in both groups of patients.

In fact, there are quite a few trials where the placebo patients had a 68% healing rate and then some other trials, randomized control trials, the treatment group has a healing rate that was substantially lower than that. So I think it's a very useful paper to read because when we talk about the placebo effect, it's certainly not the inert substance just having that effect. It's all the meaning and the symbolism and trust and connection that has it. So our colleagues that work in complementing alternative therapies I think do a much better job than us at recognizing whole people and listening to their stories.

One of the things I've been doing recently is working with professional filmmakers to interview the most incredibly inspiring health professionals and to ask them appreciative inquiry questions such as, "Tell us about a story of the most intimate connection you had with a patient or when care was most compassionate." There is an utterly compelling story told by a lady who practices homeopathy. She had patient who was infertile and been trying for many years to get pregnant, and had a lot of health problems.

It's an extraordinary story, because not only did she restore fertility to this woman in quite a short time and cure a lot of her other health problems, but the treatment that she used was profoundly symbolic of the difficulties that this patient had in life. There's a therapeutic quality to the story in the symbolism that's really profound, that I think is an important part of being a human being. That's I think what they do much better, and we just have to bring all of ourselves to the care of our patient and allow that connection to occur and bring our open hearted compassion and empathy. When I go to see a patient, I am really careful about the thoughts I have in my head, and I'm really careful about the intention I hold and I'm really careful about the suggestions I make to patients.

**Nicholas:** Because you know how powerful it is.

**Robin:** Yeah.

**Nicholas:** One of the challenges is that that doesn't go on a spreadsheet. So good doctors and nurses and ...

**Robin:** No.

**Nicholas:** ... so on, do exactly what you're talking about but they don't get any credit for it. It doesn't fit on a balanced scorecard with reds or yellows and greens and so on.

**Robin:** Yeah, if you ask your colleague, you had a relative that had an unhappy experience and you talk to the consultant doctor, if you asked him how much of your day-to-day clinical decisions, or interactions with the patients are governed by targets or a spreadsheet?" none of them at all. A lot of healthcare reform is about the setting of care and the kind of the financial compensation, none of it is about care itself. What we need to reform is care itself. The intimate nature of a relationship. The only person who can determine that is the doctor or nurse or the therapist right on the spot.

We have enormous freedom. I mean, one of the things I talk about in my book is ways in which compassionate caring can be liberated from the restrictions of the system in ways that we can just seize back power and profoundly change the way we care for patients and it creates this big influence around us.

**Nicholas:** In the kind of medical management that's prevalent in Britain, and I think in the rest of the Western world at the moment, someone in that system if they were listening to this, would say, "Great, sounds really good. Alright, well let's do it then," if they were persuaded, "Let's do it." So what we want to do is, how do we operationalize this? How do we enforce this? How do we create the systems to make this happen?

**Robin:** Yeah, yeah.

**Nicholas:** How do we measure it? How do we score it and so on? Is that possible?

**Robin:** That's an intriguing question. Can you measure compassion? In New Zealand we have a completely independent health and disability commission.

So we have a commissioner and we have a legal code of patient rights, ten points. It's in law, it's a legal code, and there's an independent commissioner appointed by parliament to uphold patients' rights and to investigate complaints. So it was interesting for us. I'm a doctor and I took a complaint to the commissioner about patient care, about our daughter's care. We just felt that her care fundamentally breached a number of her really basic rights.

In the end, the commissioner, who's actually a good friend of mine, I know him well and have worked with him in leadership roles, he was to not able to make a finding of a breach of rights. The reason for that is that he had no evidence of it, and that the only evidence he used in his inquiry was what was written in the clinical record, and the clinical record has got everything except for the patient voice.

So one of the things that we were deeply concerned about weren't on the clinical record at all. So we thought, well, if this care that was so callous and so unfeeling and so uncaring, if that doesn't cause a breach of rights then we need to change the law. So we mounted a national campaign, so every five years the legal code gets revised. So we mounted a national campaign and said, "We need to change the code of rights, and we're going to add a new right which is the right to be treated with compassion." Well, boy, that put the cat among the pigeons, because all of the professional bodies, the College of Physicians and Nurses and so on though, "Oh, crikey, now we need to make a written submission on this to the commissioner.

What do we think about it?" There were about equal numbers of submissions who were very strongly in support of that and very strongly against it. The doctors didn't like it at all. They thought their patients had too many rights already. But the commissioner had to ask the question, "Well, if we were to put this right in the legal code, how would we judge it, how would we measure it? I think it's just, it' absolutely bleeding obvious. You just ask the patient what is their emotional experience of care?

They know within two minutes whether or not care is compassionate, whether a doctor is cold and distant and controlling or whether they're empathetic and warm. It's their emotional experience. You can very easily measure it from patient experience. Now, that was one of the questions you asked me. I've forgotten the other one.

**Nicholas:** Well, if someone who is a clinician who's really inspired by what you're saying wants to become a champion for compassionate healthcare, how do you advise they go about it?

**Robin:** Okay. We're trying to create a worldwide movement, so we have a team of web programmers in Moscow and New Zealand and all sorts of countries that are working furiously, and we're building our social networking site and it's like our version of Facebook. On that site we are going to collect together from all around the world the most incredibly inspiring health professionals and students and patient advocates and health leaders who have actually undergone this transformation. They know that they can radically change their own practice, and they can change the world around them. There's a kind of bubble around each of them. They will utterly inspire you and make you see very different possibilities.

We're hoping this network will grow to be hundreds of thousands, millions across the world. There's 60 million health professionals in the world. We're only going to start with the early adopters, doctors, nurses, those that are passionate about this. There's just incredible things happening already. So come and join our community.

We're going to make it a little difficult for you. You can't just join. We really want just the committed and you're going to have to write a letter of introduction and there'll be some other barriers because to create a sustainable movement we really want people who are committed to this.

The second thing to do is just to take responsibility for your own attitude and the things that you do, the little things that you do each day. Here's a nice story. There was a senior clinician in my hospital, which at that time had a lot of challenges. They had bad patient care stories, high staff turnover, very poor morale, a challenged hospital. She came up to me one day, she saw me in the corridor and rushed up and she was quite animated and she touched my arm and said, 'Robin, Robin, I've got to tell you a story."

She said, "A couple of months ago I was referred a patient on a medical ward and she was 78 years old and she had multiple medical problems and she had angina and heart failure and she wasn't getting better and they asked me to do a specialist assessment." I sat down with her and I began to notice that she was quite anxious about something so I put down my notes and said, "I can see you're worried about something. Can you tell me what that is?" And this old lady said that she was very anxious because she really needed to phone home, like she didn't know if her dog was being fed or some circumstance, I don't know what.

Mary said, "Well, didn't you ask the nurses to use the phone?" She said, "Well, I asked for the cordless phone, but they told me every single day no, that's not for the patients, that's for the staff and you have to use the patient phone down the corridor, the card phone. She said, "Well, I'm nearly blind and I don't know how to use it." Mary said it just triggered off for her a workshop that we'd done together about little acts of kindness, and she said, "Have you got a minute?" She dashed off the ward, went down to the hospital shop, bought a ten dollar phone card with her own money, came back, took the old lady to the phone, made the phone connection, and that little old lady she cried. Because it's the first time anyone had listened to what was most important to her. Well, this took about ten minutes.

She went back to the bedside, she went back to her real job, and when she went home that day she realized she got more satisfaction out of that than anything she'd done for many months. She talked to her husband about it. She came to work the next day and she reconceptualized her notion of herself as a health professional. She said, "I'm going to be a caring human being first and an expert second." She looked each day for an opportunity for a small act of kindness. When she told me this, her eyes were shining, she was animated. She said, "Robin, it's like I have a new job." It just totally gave her meaning and a purpose back in her life, and anyone can do that.

The evidence in positive psychology is strongly supportive of that. If you do nothing else but just deliberately look for an opportunity for one small act of kindness every day, that will transform many health professionals and just open up a whole different world for you.

**Nicholas:** Thank you very much. Thank you very much Robin. That's brilliant.

**Robin:** Pleasure.

**Nicholas:** Very last thing, can you give your website address for people to look you up?

**Robin:** Ok. Two websites. The first is our international movement. It's called Hearts in Healthcare. www.heartsinhealthcare.com

You better read my book, it's just been published a month ago, and it's www.time-to-care.com. We haven't had the official launch of the book yet but it's selling like hot pancakes around the world. I've gotten offers that we can translate it into Dutch. There's quite an active group in the Netherlands that want to work with us.

**Nicholas:** Fantastic.

**Robin:** Very good.

**Nicholas:** Thank you very much Robin.

**Robin:** Pleasure. Nice to talk to you Nicholas.

# New Money

## The Evolution of Finance

**Jordan MacLeod interviewed by Dr Nicholas Beecroft**
Jordan MacLeod is a writer and consultant on the New Economy. He is author of New Currency: How Money Changes the World as We Know It and Founder and Partner of Cornerstone Global Associates, a Strategy Consulting firm based in London. Later this month he is leading cornerstone's launch of a New Economics Unit focused on re-visioning and retooling global capitalism. Jordan is also founder and CEO of a startup software company, Strue.

In this interview, Jordan puts the current economic crisis in the much bigger context of the evolution of money and financial systems throughout human history. He says,"Our economy indeed has the potential to transform into our vehicle, our shuttle, for reaching collective prosperity and increasing global integration." He traces the development of money from the tribal age of barter through to the present digital age where money has been dematerialized. Jordan doesn't claim to have a single blueprint for the future rather he has been scanning the horizon to see the evidence of our cultural evolution in action. He gives numerous examples of experimentation with new forms of currency and economic system. He gives particular focus to experiments with a method called demurrage which he believes could eliminate our compulsion for exponential growth and shift our focus towards a more co-creative and integrated society.

Jordan doesn't believe that money or capitalism are intrinsically bad, but rather our challenge is to revalue and reorganize the way we define money in a way which reflects our current and emerging values. He envisions what a more self organizing living system model of finance would look like and discusses the transition from the current system which would inevitably challenge existing power structures and vested interests. It could well be that the current global dominance of the US dollar may give way to a geopolitical shift to a Chinese-based currency or indeed a basket of multipolar currencies. Jordan thinks that it is more likely that there will be some kind of bottom-up evolution of a new global currency which will better reflect the distribution of power more broadly around the globe. He believes that this evolution of a more adaptive financial system is going to be a prime driver of our future security and way of life. He believes that the welfare system is based on entitlement in some Western countries are likely to collapse under their own weight and be replaced with something more empowering and sustainable.

**Nicholas:** Jordan MacLeod welcome to the series *Exploring The Future of Western Civilization*.

**Jordan:** Thanks Nick. Great to be here.

**Nicholas:** Jordan MacLeod is a writer and a consultant on the New Economy. He is speaking from Prince Edward Island in Canada, although a week ago he was over here in London. He is author of New Currency: How Money Changes The World as We Know It. He is writing a new book now called *Onement*. He is founder and partner of Cornerstone Global Associates which is a strategy consulting based in London. Later on this month, he is leading Cornerstone's launch of a New Economics Unit focused on re-visioning and retooling global capitalism.

Jordan is also a founder and CEO of a startup software company called Strue. Jordan, the global economy is getting through the most amazing transitional period now and it's hugely complicated for anyone to get their head around including experts in the area. I wonder if we could get just kick off by you giving your overview on how you understand it. What's actually going on?

**Jordan:** Yes, if you look at it from the global level, we're experiencing significant systemic crises. I think it's a very deep crisis that basically we're trying to solve the problems in the monetary and financial system with an old way of looking at the world. The actual limitations that we're seeing right now are extremely deep in nature. What I've been trying to show with my work is that the economy is evolving and has been evolving over centuries, millennia in a way where the subjective human nature at times comes forth and really requires a qualitative shift in the way we see the world.

In my view, the only way you can explain this crisis it is at such a deep level where we have to reconfigure not only the economic system and the external way of the monetary system works but also the way we see the world. That's something which economics in general doesn't really recognize at the moment but as this crisis goes on, I think it's going to become increasingly obvious.

**Nicholas:** Yes. Could you lay out the history of the evolution of money? What have the different stages been in the evolution of economics and can you bring that up-to-date to where we are now?

**Jordan:** When you look at the evolution of money and the qualitatively different ways of holding money and using money, there's also a component where the objective nature also changes like the way it looks and the technical aspect changes. They really correlate quite well with all of the developmental models whether it's Robert Kegan's model, *The Evolving Self* or *Spiral Dynamics* or the *Integral* view. My work has been about showing how the monetary system has evolved at each of these different stages of development and how that serves as a leverage point for further economic evolution and social evolution as a whole. It's really a critical point that I believe that we all need to be looking at carefully.

Looking back from history, you have early tribal societies. Often they didn't use money at all. Goods could have been exchanged through barter or simply through traditional mechanisms where it was more self-organizing and externally with different tribes you would have barter and often barter would even take place not in realtime but one tribe might drop off goods and then the other tribe would come and offer in return and that process would go without any face to face interaction because of the lack of communication.

As money evolves, it's gone from found objects like cowry shells, or rocks, or et cetera and then towards things like even cows which were considered to be the first form of money. There's an organic process from barter into money and as it goes, it evolves through the ability to create money. Aristotle pointed out that the ability to create money goes hand-in-hand with the ability to create empires. The money was initially created through the value intrinsic to the coins made from precious metals and a base metal later on, but as things have evolved over the last few hundred years we have evolved to a Gold Standard and then to now to monetarism where money isn't backed by gold or any other object.

Right now, we're in this half-baked situation where we are off the Gold Standard but at the same time we haven't really created the mechanisms that ensure the stability of a monetary supply beyond some limited parameters. There's a strong yearning to go back to the Gold Standard and the security of that. One of the arguments that I'm trying to make is that we're evolving beyond the Gold Standard toward an increasing dematerialization of money and value of money.

As money has evolved, I think that the quality that we're seeing is that it's increasing in span. As it's changing towards digital money especially we're seeing the capacity to go from a limited tribal value towards a global scale, the span, but is also an increasing depth at each exchange as well. I think that's something that is critical for us to understand right now when there's such a dysfunction between the macro and micro and the feelings of disempowerment at the community level. There's a strong movement towards community currencies and to supporting resilience in communities which is an extraordinarily valid movement but we can't forego and forget about the global and the systemic alignment as well, which is a very complex challenge.

**Nicholas:** You're saying that each of these different evolutionary stages of finance relates to the life conditions and the cultural development at a particular time in a particular place. What is it that's driving the change now? Why is it that the system that we have did work but is now challenged and needs to adapt?

**Jordan:** I think it's just the global nature of finance on the one hand. I think that you can look at that from many different angles. You look at the West and from an objective point of view when you look at the unprecedented wealth creation and technology and levels of the highest standards of living in history, you would think that we had it all figured out but then when you look at the extraordinarily high depression rates, unemployment, poverty, the base levels, there's something going on where it just isn't creating a society that we had hoped to have attained by the time we've had the material part figured out.

**Nicholas:** Yes.

**Jordan:** The pursuit of happiness has gone off the rails a little bit here and I think that we need to reevaluate that. So that's one aspect of it. The other aspect is the global financial system where you really need overt global regulation and a global body to ensure that the system isn't abused. Right now we're seeing the inability of the different regulating bodies of the nation state to reign in the speculative forces that are operating on a global level. That also applies to taxation and it could be up to a trillion dollars a year that's lost in taxation throughout the world through offshore banking and so on. It's a huge number though at a global level and all of this is something we need to look at.

**Nicholas:** If we fast forward to the future, do you have a particular vision of how it should be or could be to be successful?

**Jordan:** The way that I'm looking at it in the new book is applying Hayek's view in The Road to Serfdom. That book had a really strong impact me at a younger age in looking at his defense of capitalism versus stronger degrees of centralization and the arbitrary power of dictators and beliefs that spawned in that sort of socialization models. What I came to realization of is that his view can block the evolution as well if we take the position that we're at the highest level and we've done away with arbitrary power for example.

Whereas I think if we have an evolutionary view, we're saying that we're at one stage and we have to confront and bring to light the arbitrariness and the arbitrary power, arbitrary structures that exist currently. The future is something that has confronted that and is something that has built a monetary system and a financial system that will be characterized by decentralization and a greater, qualitatively different level of self-organization. It's transcended specific financial issues that are limiting emergence today.

**Nicholas:** Right. I'd like to give a quote from your book. You talk about a powerful perceptual shift that you personally had years ago when you saw this picture called *Onement* in an art gallery here in London and I know from when we met last week, you'd just gone back to see the artist. In your book you link that to a huge shift in the way you saw the world and then you say, "Our economy has the potential to transform into a vehicle, our shuttle for reaching collective prosperity and increasing global integration." That's a huge leap from a picture to that amazing vision. How does that all fit together?

**Jordan:** Well, the painting, that was about 12 years ago when I was in London, living in London and just happened to walk into this art gallery and the painting was a reference to an artist, a New York artist. The painting had rope going from top to the bottom. It's a painting with Goyaesque figures sticking out of there. There was something that really connected me to just my own suffering and to our collective suffering that was quite strong and disturbing. As I was holding that painting, it also brought me to a space where I experienced really for the first time a feeling of oneness, of integration and peace that I had really never even considered possible before.

**Nicholas:** Just from looking at a painting?

**Jordan:** Yes, from this painting. I was really catalyzed by this painting and so it really set me on a course of trying to understand that in the economics system. If that was an experiential reality that was valid then surely there were structures that could be eventually created. It could take a long time. It should be a theoretical and structural mechanism to reinforce that reality and to bringing forth that reality in society. That was why it set the whole process in motion and *Onement* the title of the painting had really been a living symbol for me in terms of how I think about the world and I look at that word holographically.

I really apply it to myself and also at the macro scale as well and so I've come to understand that as a gradual process of evolution where we're taking steps, baby steps at times and often a step backward but on the grand trajectory there's a movement towards oneness. In the monetary system, that's something that I believe the next step would be catalyzed by a tool that we call demurrage and that is something that I think will help achieve greater integration and interconnectivity and I guess a market economy that also reinforces our cooperative nature as well.

**Nicholas:** Before I read your book, I hadn't heard of that term, "Demurrage." Could you explain that?

**Jordan:** Yes, it was an idea that was originated by Silvio Gesell who was a German merchant who he spent a lot of time in Argentina and Europe trying to understand the economic system and why we're so susceptible to boom and bust cycles and to collapse. He developed this concept over time, published a book called *The Natural Economic Order* and it led to the application of this concept which is taxing money in a way that it leads us to create money that mirrors the natural world and its decay and the cost of keeping things fresh, alive, safe, basically a timing for the cost of overcoming the second law of thermodynamics.

The idea of demurrage in the day was endorsed by John Maynard Keynes and Irving Fisher and several of the towering economic figures of the Twentieth century. However there really wasn't the mechanism to apply that on a broad scale. It was successful in a limited version in the town of Worgl in Austria during the great depression. It completely revitalized and reenergized the town in a short period of time. Then it became known as the miracle of Worgl and heads of nations from all over the world were visiting to understand it. It was shut down by Hitler and the Nazis. I guess you could say it wasn't necessarily encouraged elsewhere as well. In the US, I think there was a fear of competing monetary systems and with the New Deal there was a push towards centralized power and to doing whatever they had to do to stabilize a very weak economy.

**Nicholas:** Why would the people there have agreed to trade in a currency or be paid in a currency which decays over time rather than in one that doesn't? Who would choose that?

**Jordan:** I think that there's a lot of different ways you can look at that. I think first of all we all pay for the operation of our monetary system anyhow through taxation. It's always externalized. By internalizing the cost of the system, then the money holders themselves become responsible for operating a system. What it does is it penalizes hoarding and ensures that money continues to flow throughout the economy stably and that benefits everyone.

It benefits lenders because of the stronger circulation. It benefits borrowers because it tends to over time push interest rates down and there are other benefits whereas these interest rates go down it tends to benefit in a multitude of ways. It mitigates the systemic compulsion for exponential growth which is putting pressure on our global ecology and also psyche for basically producing more goods that have diminishing value and return. It also reduces the concentration of wealth effects and generally stabilizes the economy.

The more the interest rates are dissolved through this process, which is essentially saturating capital markets it also creates a mechanism where nations with very different economic conditions can operate within the same system. That's a critical component of what we're seeing in Greece right now because within the EU you have a single interest rate and monetary policy for very different economies. That is one of the reasons why several economists were able to predict that in the medium term, the Euro would fail and that's been predictable for more than a decade.

**Nicholas:** Yes, well anyone with common sense, not caught up in the wishful thinking groupthink would have predicted that. Effectively we have demurrage anyway because inflation eats away at your money so the value of your money does decay through time already so we already have that system effectively.

**Jordan:** It's qualitatively different. The way I explain it in the book, it's a qualitatively different dynamic but it's still the same process. The way I compare it is to the denial of death. I think that at a cultural level, our aversion to accounting for the second law, third law dynamics in the money is really is a function of actually of narcissism, a denial of death and our disconnection from nature.

The monetary system is actually a reflection of our consciousness and how that is now, in turn, being reinforced by the economic system against even our intentions. It's comparable to death. Whether we're denying that or whether we're consciously accepting of it, it's going to happen anyway. I think that this is similar in that inflation and demurrage are very similar processes but one is a conscious application of an understanding where the other is the side effect that in fact diminishes our capacity to prosper.

That's something that economists are even starting to understand and you know inflation is actually being embraced to some degree now and that's obviously scary if it goes beyond a certain limit but, within reason, I think there's more of an appetite for some inflation to get ahead of this. Ultimately it's not a process that is dynamic enough. It really leads to a completely different qualitative characteristics of the economy.

**Nicholas:** I always found money quite funny because everyone acts as if its true and real and we really do need it in order to survive actually but in another sense it doesn't even exist. It only exists because we all agree it exists. It's like a shared trick. It is like a magical fantasy. It's true as long as everyone believes it.

**Jordan:** Yes.

**Nicholas:** I wonder if we push that forwards, could you imagine companies like cable and wireless or telecommunication companies, they show these pictures of globe with all the different cables or lines connected. Imagine that you could see the flow of financial capital around the world like that which is happening as a continuous flow like a kind of self-organizing living system, if the whole global civilization was a living being like a complex vast rain forest.

If we imagine money as a store or a marker for human energy and investments are actual human potential. You could actually imagine that money is the flow of human energy into human potential does that make sense?

**Jordan:** Yes, I think it does. The visualization of what you're talking about it could be really powerful. If you could show how money is flowing throughout the global system, the way it's concentrating and also the way it turns itself off. When you're talking about the flow of energy and you think about hoarding, and think about blocking that energy, there's something really invaluable in understanding that. The more we're willing to let it go and to keep it flowing then the more resilient system becomes and everyone's energy level will increase.

That energy is right now flowing to the global financial capitals of the world, the London's, the Tokyo's and the New York's, and in the new system we can visualize that being far more decentralized. There's just a win-win situation where that money is flowing and coming back when you need it as opposed to hoarding it and building on it through interest rates.

I also think it's important to visualize collectively how that stops flowing. Yes it's flowing today and we've a lot of tools that are being used to keep it moving, quantitative easing for example, lowering interest rates at central banks. When there's a severe economic crisis or financial crisis, money stops moving. That's when you really start to see the value of this tool because there's a willingness to let go and to get things moving again from a global level.

**Nicholas:** If we're looking at the global financial system as a conscious living system, there's a logic to that. If you take an axe to a tree or burn a tree or something like that, the tree's natural internal systems will actually cut bits off and that's a healthy thing. In a human if you chop a finger off or something, the blood supply shuts down to protect the whole, because otherwise you're going to bleed to death. If they're bad investments, you don't want to throw all the human energy into the bad, throw good money after bad.

**Jordan:** Correct. Exactly, I think there's two different ways of looking at it. I think at a global level it'll be more, the analogy will be more of a cardiac arrest or the actual heart as a whole stops pumping so the blood or the money supply isn't flowing at all.

**Nicholas:** Right.

**Jordan:** At the same time you don't want to be forcing, like you said, you don't want be forcing money unnaturally into areas that are poor investments. What you're really looking at doing is reconfiguring the market itself to operate in a way that internalizes the cost of storing the money supply and that in turn creates a new logic that makes sense and it's qualitatively different.

**Nicholas:** One of the things you've done in researching your book and your business as well is looking across the world at the different kind of experiments that people are doing, the people of the cutting edge, the evolutionary edge of the global financial system, trying out new ideas, trying out new methods and models. I wonder if you could talk about a few of those that you've seen the most promising.

**Jordan:** Well, one of the ones that I think are really interesting is Bitcoin. That's an open source monetary system and form of money that is peer-to-peer. Basically there is no central authority. It has a design. It has a fixed number of units that are being created and everybody has a bit of the monetary system operating on their computer. It's capable of authenticating trade transactions, unique transactions in a way that's proven very successful. What's fascinating about this system is the fact that it's completely self-organizing but also the fact that it has very clear design flaws to it but the open nature of it allows the people to look to move in and to innovate and to solve those problems really quickly.

**Nicholas:** I didn't quite grasp how it works and what's the currency in Bitcoin.

**Jordan:** Bitcoin is technically backed by cycles of processing power but it's really just an online digital currency that is operating through a peer-to-peer network of individuals. There's nobody really producing units of this currency. There is no central power who are assigning interest rates or anything like that. It's basically self-organizing by design.

**Nicholas:** It's a closed system. Someone creates a fixed number of units and then those units can be traded?

**Jordan:** Yes. That's one of the design problems to it because there's no relationship between supply and demand. It's leading to bubbles and there's some relative instability in price but it does have a relationship with other forms of currency like other national currency so it's working to some degree as a mechanism for exchange rate, basically carrying out international currency trading. It has enormous power. I think when you look at peer-to-peer currencies and where that may head, it could be the most disruptive and empowering monetary innovation in history. There are obviously clear design problems to it so if those can get resolved then it's something that could be phenomenal.

**Nicholas:** Yes.

**Jordan:** One thing I want to just talk about was that there are developers that are working on integrating demurrage into the system. It's really important to visualize because if you internalize the cost of operating monetary system and you have demurrage then you have this basically collective ability to create new solutions to the design problems where you're able to aggregate some money to basically build what you need to make it self-organizing. You can design and then resolve the problem of issuing credits, creating an algorithm that is non-arbitrary so everybody can benefit.

**Nicholas:** Going back to the power and the evolutionary thing, you said that Aristotle said that the ability to create money is linked to the ability to create an Empire. Money and power are intrinsically linked. How is that going to work out in the transition from where we are? There may have been, we've got central banks and governments that create money. Within that, as the occupy people keep saying, a relatively small number of people and institutions have a great deal of power.

If you imagine fast forwarding to sort of a much more living-system-based interconnected world in which the hierarchies are much flatter that's going to be a challenge to a lot of vested interests. How's that transition going to work and why would those vested interests agree to it, and who has the power to make that happen?

**Jordan:** Yes, that's really the question. When you look at central banks right now, they are over their heads. I think they know it and they're basically are in the business of keeping this system together. When you look at the Euro in particular, it's just an exhausting process for central banks and for politicians that occupies all of their time. It's a perpetual crisis now. As we're seeing now it's moving in Spain and we're seeing multibillion dollar, we are looking at up to 100 billion dollars to bail out the Spanish banks. It's difficult to foresee this reversing any time soon. They stand as much to win by this as the crisis goes on as anybody and to show how this can be self-organizing will be a relief frankly to central banks.

**Nicholas:** What would that look like in a European Context? What's the structure you're talking about?

**Jordan:** It could go down any ways. The easiest way for this to happen and the most peaceful way would certainly need to be some sort of alignment of vision between the central bankers and the grassroots movements like Occupy. If the movement is creative, then I think that's certainly possible. We tend to think of central banks as being out of touch and trying to maintain a status quo but I'm not convinced that's the case. As I said, Keynes and others that proposed this idea for almost a century and it was considered impossible in the day to really implement it but now with digital currency it's something that we can do quite easily.

The way that I conceptualize it is that in the book that I'm writing after *Onement* is called *Ego, Money, Empire* and looking at these different structures as really deeply interconnected and all three of them are evolving. They are all mediating our sense of separation and the need to create order and make sense to the world so the inherent need to create structure, but as they evolve, they increasingly decentralize, they increasingly dissolve in a sense and become less of our sense of identity and more of a vehicle and a tool that we can use.

Empire and Ego, I think, can both, for people in spiritual movements, and the integral movement, can have really strong negative associations but as we see it as a tool, it can become something that is actually an enlightened process as well. Something that isn't shunned, glorified or shunned.

**Nicholas:** That's a great point. I mean an awful lot of people have a got a feeling about money and about the financial system that it's somehow dirty, it's wrong, it's inherently bad. Some people say it's a conspiracy or there are small groups that manipulate the whole and so on. For example, one chap who calls himself a true communist, he asked me to ask you if every human being has their basic needs means of being fed, food, security, water, education, love, and so on why would anyone want any money. Why not just get rid of money altogether? Why do we need a financial system?

**Jordan:** Yes. I guess there're a few different ways of looking at that. When you look at that, it really becomes a philosophical issue and why we're here and why we're on this earth. What he's saying is that we have some sort of nanny state to look after us and to provide what we need and if we've that then everything will be fine. I think that is diametrically the opposite direction of where we're heading.

We're heading in a place where we're creating a system that is allowing us to fish for ourselves, basically allowing us to evolve, to grow, and to develop the skills that we need to find a deep meaning in our lives. If anything, in the West, what we're seeing is that having our material need satisfied isn't enough. There's a really strong impulse to find a deeper meaning and that's something the state will never be able to provide and any sort of collectivist ideology will never be able to provide.

What's critical is that, what you were saying earlier, as money being perceived as being evil that's the challenge. What we have right now is the system that it reflective of human values and a way of living in the world that really doesn't resonate with a lot of people. There's a strong misalignment between a monetary system on the one hand and how people want things to be, and so there's a tendency to throw out the baby with the bath water, wanting to get rid of money entirely rather than to see it as an evolutionary vehicle and to see that it is possible to change the relationship with that.

**Nicholas:** How can we change the way we use money or the way we value investments and assets to reflect a broader range of human values then?

**Jordan:** Well, that's the interesting thing about interest rates and demurrage. The more we're able to dissolve the interest rates through the saturation of capital markets, that inherently increases the incentive to favor longer term investment so that alone, overcoming discounted cash flow, that essentially dictates that it's better to have to make money now and to have to make money now than to have money in the future.

If that process changes then what you're doing is rewarding longer term thinking on investments, longer term deeper investments, more capital intensive investments and also collaborative investments. It begins to reward longer term thinking and also integrated thinking where you're not looking for a short term solution. When you think of companies moving all over the world just to save money and leaving the former community in the dust, that sort of thing will be less and less common as it's more of a mutual win-win incentive in that process.

**Nicholas:** I suppose we see that in embryo already because, for example, a pension fund will be much more cautious and long term in its way of investing compared to a sort of a get-rich-quick individual.

**Jordan:** Yes. When you look at the new jobs bill in US and the crowdfunding legislation that's coming forward right now, we're right at the beginning of an entirely new funding mechanism where companies can be funded at a much lower level scale, with crowdfunding, it can be thousands of people funding up to 2 million dollars at $100 of investment. It can be at a very small level whereas before you had to have couple of million dollars to be accredited to invest.

**Nicholas:** Where's that working well at the moment, Jordan? Where's that got off the ground?

**Jordan:** Well, it isn't really working anywhere yet. As far as I understand, it's completely a new way of doing it. It's a completely new investment model that doesn't exist anywhere at any large scale. I think the US will be the first to be successful in doing it. Just staying in Europe a couple weeks ago, I had the chance to talk to a few of the companies who are creating platforms to enable these sort of investments. I think it's really exciting. I think it's going to create a far stronger relationship between the 99% and creative entrepreneurs. That's going to be global scale as well. That's the way the energy is also starting to flow in new ways.

**Nicholas:** (laughing) You can see how that will unleash a whole new load of forces. I'm chuckling because it will also open up a whole new range of options for scams and bubbles and manipulators and dodgy information and so on.

**Jordan:** Absolutely, that's going to be the case against doing crowdfunding. It's going to increase the value of reputation, transparency, assets information and basically a stronger relationship between investors and the founding members of the new enterprise. That's going to be fascinating. It's going to be something that is very different from what we see in large corporations and shareholders.

**Nicholas:** Yes. That'll be Interesting to watch. You mentioned earlier local currencies. Are any of these working well?

**Jordan:** Well, my favorite regional or community currency is the Chiemgauer that's in Germany and basically what they're doing is that they're hacking the Euro with a demurrage system built on top of it. It's actually a regional currency that's backed by the Euro. There is a one-to-one relationship so they're really interchangeable. Because of the demurrage rate, it is encouraging and incentivizing the flow of money much faster through the economy so it's effectively circulating twice as fast. It is circulating twice as fast as the Euro in that region and which effectively doubles the money supply. It's a very creative way to enhance the potential for regional prosperity. If you apply that at the global level then obviously the money supply will simply be inflationary but what really matters is that the qualitatively different relationship with money and encourages different behaviors.

**Nicholas:** It's the speed of flow of money that increases?

**Jordan:** And the stability of circulation and also the way it rewards different behaviors and economic decisions.

**Nicholas:** There are underlying geopolitical shifts. We've still got the legacy of the American dollar as the global currency and that has stretched well beyond the conditions that originally set that up. It's still running because it suits everyone but eventually there will come some challenge to the system or the Chinese, the Arabs and the Russians will eventually get together and pull the rug on that.

When that happens, do you think that that will simply be a descent into chaos, a backward step and simply a shift of power from one bunch of people to another or is it going to be an opportunity for a higher level global currency that serves everyone better?

**Jordan:** Yes that's exactly, yes. Your question really summarizes the situation really well because what we're seeing is the American dollar functioning as a global currency. It's extremely difficult to sustain it in a multipolar geopolitical dynamic where China is emerging, the BRIC countries in general are emerging. What we might say is the risk of a decline in Europe, financial and economic decline and possibly in America as well with the rise of the East and all of these different nations. What we're seeing is the potential for real competition to assert from different nations and perhaps regions to assert themselves as the top dog and to replace the dollar.

That to me is also the impetus for the qualitative evolution that you're talking, that you mentioned because when you look at central banks within the illusion of the status quo today, there is an illusion that everything is stable and will stay the way it is for a long time but as we see this competition between Russia, China, different countries that don't really represent Western values, Western countries including the central banks will be forced to take a decision that will either be do these countries assert themselves within the current paradigm and take control from US or are we moving to something completely different? The more that question becomes apparent, the more unstable the financial system becomes and the more we see these sort of geopolitical races and jousting for position. What we're seeing is this ground up movement embodied in Occupy and many other places could emerge as another alternative. That's what's new will be forced and whether that's regressive or evolutionary.

**Nicholas:** PayPal is an online trading system really isn't it? It would presumably be just the flick of a switch and a bit of programming work to create a global currency with that kind of platform. Why hasn't that happened yet?

**Jordan:** I think that at some level you need the cooperation of the nation states and ideally their willingness to work together to create a global body that makes things much easier to regulate. When you look at the US for example, creating a new monetary platform or anything basically requires accreditation in every single state so the legal processes are overwhelming. They can be extremely expensive and a real barrier to entry.

PayPal for example it makes money largely through currency exchange between national currencies and small fees for transaction elsewhere but that particular platform isn't really geared I don't think for evolving per se. You would need a more open system that allows for monetary innovation, that's the really vision of the Austrian Economist who believed in competition between currencies.

However that really runs against the central bank model where you have a currency and you have control over that currency and you have ability to a large degree to maintain the supply and demand relationship. It's where they're unable to manage that that's really where the paradigmatic and systemic problems come in.

**Nicholas:** At the core it's a combination of power and trust isn't it? Whoever is in charge of a currency whether they're a country or a company or a community, they've got to have sufficient control over the resources and institutions and people to be able to enforce its credibility and people have got to trust them for the currency to be credible.

**Jordan:** There has to be a proven performance as well over time. We can talk about these ideas all day but really it comes to whether they work and how well they work. That's something that you proved by building it and over time gaining confidence. What we'll find is that not only do they work but they also help us transcend some of the mental blocks that we have when it comes to the split between the left versus the right and the high polarization in political processes and also the top down and bottom up of the economy as well. The more we're able to fold both sides of these issues in the interest of both, I think the more peaceful and conscious the transformation will be.

**Nicholas:** I sometimes think when we look back at history, I'm sure all generations do this, we have this idea that we're really advanced and look back on previous cultures or previous periods in history and think how could they possibly do that, like slavery being a really obvious example of something which to us is totally unacceptable and it's hard to imagine people's thought processes behind that, but if we fast forward into the future, there'll be a lot of the things that we do currently that future generations will look back at and think, "what the hell were they doing? How could they be so stupid?" I wonder is there anything in our financial system that's like that? For example, I wonder whether we'll look back this notion of having debt as being form of slavery, a mortgage as being a chain around your neck and the slavery having to have the money go into your bank account from the company you work for?

**Jordan:** Yes, I don't know about that. The interest on money can be more of an enslaving function because you're basically working extra to service that debt over time and obviously a 10% interest rate will double every seven years so that creates an enormous pressure from the borrowers point of view. Some individuals have access to lower rates now and certainly helps but we see situations where even 20 years ago, these rates were getting to 20% and that's really impossible to pay a mortgage from something get that high, as opposed to if you're used to a lower rate and your income is relatively constant. In coming to your question about how future generations might look back I think one thing will be this compulsion we have to grow at all costs and the diminishing returns; basically working harder and harder and putting increasing pressure on ourselves to grow and to build goods of diminishing value. That aspect of it I think is really something that we'll be amazed to see how in the process of waking up to basically the impact that we have on the whole of life and on entire ecosystem and the way the economic system and structure has material impact on our consciousness and our mental state and seeing individual actors not aligned with the whole whether you can characterize that as narcissism, sociopathic behavior whatever.

I'm sure there are lot of terms that could be applied but it's really just that misalignment between the individual and the whole and it's devastating impact on the planet. I think that future generations will appreciate the enormous difficulty of the challenge we're in and waking up to it I'm sure they'll have a lot of gratitude for us doing so.

**Nicholas:** We use money to buy things, we also use money to redistribute wealth. If you look at the way that many Western countries, definitely in Europe and Canada, have quite big welfare systems and currently have an apartheid between people who work and earn money and those people who are in dependency states some of whom get into entitlement mentality although, of course, entitlement exists at all levels of society. A lot of the dark side of that human nature plays out with that. Is anyone experimenting as far as you know with better ways of doing what we currently call welfare so as to be empowering rather than disempowering and to inspire responsibility and freedom as opposed to entitlement and resentment.

**Jordan:** No I can't. I can't think of anything, any country or anywhere where that is actually being applied but what you're is saying is exactly where we're heading. I think the nature of a more self-organizing economy requires an engagement by individuals. It's a double-edged sword. When you look at Worgl for example that applied demurrage, they attained full employment in the middle of the great depression in a relatively quick period of time.

I think the opportunity for employment will be there for people capable of working and interested in working and the centralization of power and bureaucracy in government are going to dissolve over time and those mechanisms for support will be carried out much more the by the community itself and, in a way, that aspect is back to the future. Communities were much stronger let's say a 100 years ago than they are today. Certainly, there was a willingness for neighbors to help each other out and that's certainly still true as well no doubt but the entitlement aspect is going to collapse under its own weight.

The way that welfare is carried out right now simply isn't sustainable and as these financial systems begin to collapse, we're already seeing it in Europe, I don't think there's anyway that that's going to continue. There's a real urgent need to create mechanisms that bring people in. At the national level and internationally there has to be a new, really a new evolutionary truth, a new dynamic between individuals co-creator, helping each other to grow to build meaningful lives, to find what it is that they really value and to act on that. That has to be something that is extremely creative. It has to be something that provides new opportunities at a tangible level as well.

When you look at the Middle East I think there has to be just a qualitative shift there as well in terms of economic opportunity to help soften some of the rigid ideologies.

**Nicholas:** I was traveling in Syria once very close to the border with Israel with the British Ambassador. He was pointing out just how close all the different places are there. Beirut was just over the mountains, we could see Israel ahead of us. Many of the great cities of the Middle East would be within a few hours drive if that were politically possible such as in Canada or America. I'd just got back from Minnesota and San Francisco. If you put this region it in that kind of place it would be a tiny little area. It would be full of giant highways and motorways and service stations with one currency and people wouldn't be worried about old fashioned tribal and religious hostilities. They'd be just getting on and living their lives really but that's very easy to say but is there any way you could use the financial system and the economic system in that region to shift people priorities and consciousness in a way so that the conflict fell away and became less important?

**Jordan:** I think that is an extremely difficult question. When you look at that region, when you look at countries like Iran and in Egypt, other countries like Syria as well, there's a real disconnect between the people and the leadership. You need some sort of mechanism that increases their opportunity to live meaningful lives. That's essentially the origins of the Arab Spring as well. When you look at the merchant who set himself on fire because he was being abused and mocked and prevented from making a decent living, that's a real function of the situation they're in.

Anything that is more integrative that enables economic participation across national levels, it's something that will really shift their area of focus and ideally catalyze new energy and ability to tap into their energy that right now is blocked. When you look at the unemployment levels of a bulging young generation in their early 20s and teenage years it's critical for them to have a creative outlet otherwise it will turn destructive.

**Nicholas:** Yes. Yes. That was pointed out by Neil Howe in one of the previous interviews in this series. He's predicting in about 15 years some really dramatic changes as the generations shifts in the Middle East.

A couple of last final thoughts. There is big inequality in wealth within both within western countries and between the rich countries and the poor countries. Does that matter?

**Jordan:** The world that we're living in is extremely complex. It is what it is. The more we're able to create a system that enables everyone to make a decent living, to take charge of their economic destiny and to empower not only themselves but those around them, the better off we're going to be. I think that we need to frame this in the geopolitical and the historical context of where we are. I think that it can't usefully be framed as the rise and fall of the West and the basically the reassertion of Russia and China and the East.

That paradigm of hierarchies itself is eroding. It really is a situation where there is a potential win-win-win for all of us if we're able to create a system that works for everyone. That's something that can sound Utopian but at a pragmatic level we can't settle for anything less and I do think that it's increasingly possible and it's just simply a matter of intention and execution.

**Nicholas:** If anyone listening wants to keep abreast of the evolutionary edge of finance where people are experimenting, trying out new things and to see the latest developments, where would they look?

**Jordan:** That's a great question. I think the number of different individuals working on monetary issues and I don't know if there's one central place to go. Charles Eisenstein has some great ideas about demurrage and money, Bernard Lietaer, Thomas Greco, there's a lot of people, peer-to-peer movement in general has a lot of interest in this area. It really depends on where one resonates, I guess.

**Nicholas:** Finally, what we've been talking about can feel enormous for us as individuals. What are you doing with your own money and how are you personally making your own decisions to adapt to what is already fast changing environment?

**Jordan:** I'm putting in almost all of my money into creating a software company and consulting company with a focus, my personal focus being on the New Economics Unit and really wanting to build the systems that work and so that's where my money's going and ideally that will be something that emerges as part of the solution.

**Nicholas:** Thank you so much Jordan. It's been a real pleasure to speak with you.

**Jordan:** Thanks Nick, I appreciate it.

**Nicholas:** Very last point, if someone wants to read your present book or your future books and get in touch with you, have a look at your new IT startup, how will they do that?

**Jordan:** They can go to cstoneglobal.com to visit our consulting company or the actual software startup.

**Nicholas:** The book is ...

**Jordan:** New Currency and that's available at Amazon and different book stores.

**Nicholas:** Fantastic. Thank you very much Jordan.

**Jordan:** Thanks Nick.

**Nicholas:** Cheerio.

**Jordan:** Cheers.

# Other Books in the Series

The Future of Western Civilization series is available in four books in paperback and ebook. Each interview is also available as a separate ebook. You will find them on the main online book retailers.

www.FutureofWesternCivilization.com

## Future of Western Civilization Series 1, Book 1

### Introduction to the Series

### British Patriotism
*A Newcomer's Perspective*

### The Next Big Shift
*From Machine to Living System*

### Global Simultaneous Policy Making
*Bottom-Up Global Policy*

### The Future of Capitalism
*Getting What We Really Want*

### Transpartisan Politics
*The Power of Integrating Diversity*

### Creating Heaven on Earth
*Taking Small Steps in the Right Direction*

### Bonds, Fields and Intentions
*Culture Catches Up with Science*

### Leadership with Integrity
*How to be True to Yourself*

### Wisdom
*Lost and Rediscovered*

### The Living Universe
*Bringing Science, Finance and Society to Life*

### Organizational Democracy
*10 Steps to Democratic Culture and Leadership*

## Future of Western Civilization Series 1, Book 2

**The West is Best**
*Insights from the PR Man to the Stars*

**Evolutionary Enlightenment**
*Living from your Creative Impulse*

**Renaissance 2**
*Catalyzing the Second Renaissance.*

**Positive Patriotism**
*The Evolving British*

**The Master Code**
*The Theory that Explains Everything*


## Future of Western Civilization Series 1, Book 4

**Unleashing Human Potential**
*Alignment, Energetics and Connection*

**Wise Democracy**
*Discovering Solutions to Intractable Problems*

**Mindfulness**
*Applications for Leaders and Clinicians*

**Evolutionary Leadership**
*Conscious Leadership in an Age of Transition*

**The Future of Europe**
*A View from Inside the European Union*

**Ending the Culture War**
*A Devoted Conservative and a Die-hard Liberal Make Friends*

**The Future of Western Civilization Progress Report**

# Contact & Social Media

Thank you so much for reading the Future of Western Civilization. Please do get in touch to share your comments. Please visit the web-sites below.

www.FutureofWesternCivilization.com

www.nicholasbeecroft.com

http://www.facebook.com/groups/438696922812104/

http://twitter.com/Future_of_West

http://www.linkedin.com/groups?gid=4400956

# Write a review

If you really enjoyed the book and the series, then please do tell your friends, share on social media and do please post reviews on Amazon, Goodreads, Kobo, Barnes & Noble, Sony, Smashwords etc. It'll help others decide whether to get a copy for themselves. If you have found any typos, awful grammar or anything else I can put right, please email me directly and I'll do so.

Best wishes,
Nicholas

www.ingramcontent.com/pod-product-compliance
Lightning Source LLC
Chambersburg PA
CBHW070901290526
45795CB00001B/194